Periodic Supplement #4

THE MINISTER'S LIBRARY

Cyril J. Barber

BAKER BOOK HOUSE
Grand Rapids, Michigan 49506

BARBER, Cyril John, 1934-   016.2
The Minister's Library, by Cyril J. Barber.
Grand Rapids: Baker Book House, 1978.
p.; 26cm.
(Periodic supplement; 4). Includes index.
[Z7751] ISBN: 0-8010-0813-1 pbk.:
1. Religion—Bibliography. 2. Theological
libraries. I. Title.
Copyright 1982 by Baker Book House Company
Printed in the United States of America

Contents

Preface

1. General Reference Works 1
2. Bible 5
3. Old Testament 9
4. New Testament 15
5. Doctrinal Theology 25
6. Devotional Literature 33
7. Marriage and Family Living 39
8. Pastoral Theology 47
9. Missions 57
10. Christian Education 59
11. Church History and Biography 61
12. Comparative Religions and Cults 65
    Author Index 67
    Title Index 72

Contents

Preface

The tokens of appreciation on the part of those who are in the ministry and have used *The Minister's Library* and its supplements has prompted the issue of this supplement, thus bringing the catalog of books published up to December 1980.

This volume has been produced under very difficult circumstances and the pressures of my regular occupation have never been felt to quite the same extent. In this connection, however, I am most fortunate to have had the services of Mrs. Les (Ellen) Beery who, on very short notice, undertook the typing of the manuscript. To her I owe a very sincere word of thanks.

I would also like to thank the editorial and production personnel of Baker Book House for their constant encouragement and unfailing helpfulness in preparing these biennial supplements for publication.

Finally, I would like to express my sincere thanks to my dear wife, Aldyth, for her support over so many years of ministry.

Cyril J. Barber

Chapter 1

GENERAL REFERENCE WORKS

Books regarded as most important and worthy of acquisition have been marked with an asterisk (*). Those of general interest are included for the sake of readers who desire to read broadly in a particular area. Books espousing a theological viewpoint that is not in keeping with a conservative, evangelical position have been identified with a dagger (†). This does not necessarily mean that they are not worthy of consultation or acquisition. It does avoid repetition of annotations in regard to this point.

Bible

Anderson, David A. *All the Trees and Woody Plants of the Bible*. Waco, TX: Word Books, 1979.

After years of service in the U.S. Forestry Service and five trips to the Middle East, Anderson has brought his experience to bear on the trees and shrubs mentioned in the Bible. The result is a handy, well-indexed volume. 220.8'58.AN2

Bromiley, G. W., et al., eds. *The International Standard Bible Encyclopedia*, Vol. 1, A-D. Grand Rapids: Wm. B. Eerdmans Publishing Co., 1979.

Originally published in 1915 and revised in 1929, this work is now in the process of fresh revision. Based on the RSV, it now includes articles on every person and place mentioned in the Bible. Some articles have been retained from the earlier edition. The contributors, however, are not all conservative theologians, and the difference of viewpoint is evident. Well illustrated and beautifully produced. 220.3.IN8B v.1

*****Douglas, J. D., et al.**, eds. *The Illustrated Bible Dictionary*. 3 vols. Wheaton, IL: Tyndale House Publishers, 1980.

Formerly published as the *New Bible Dictionary*, this new, revised, up-dated, and lavishly illustrated work retains many of the excellencies of the older work. Some of the articles in the former edition have been omitted, and others merged with similar topics for easier reference. Coverage is excellent; the dates of certain OT events tend to reflect the opinion of liberal scholarship; the index in vol. 3 is most helpful and complete. Timely, helpful, and exceptionally well produced. 220.3.IL6 1980

Wright, J. Stafford. *Revell's Dictionary of Bible People*. Old Tappan, NJ: Fleming H. Revell Company, 1978.

Covers Bible personalities from Aaron to Zophar. Each entry is accompanied by the meaning of the name (where known) and a brief summary of the biblical data about them. Handy. 220.92.W93

Old Testament

*****Botterwick, G. Johannes**, and **Helmer Ringgren**, eds. *Theological Dictionary of the Old Testament*. Vol. IV. Translated by D. E. Green. Grand Rapids: Wm. B. Eerdmans Publishing Co., 1980.

†This essential work covers $z^e ebh$ to *hms*, emphasizes Hebrew terminology and biblical usage, considers each word in light of its cognates, and provides an abundance of material for both pastor and teacher. 221.4'4.B65 v.4

*Harris, Robert Laird; Gleason Leonard Archer, Jr., and Bruce Kenneth Waltke, eds. *Theological Wordbook of the Old Testament.* 2 vols. Chicago: Moody Press, 1980.

Less comprehensive than *Theologisches Wörterbuch zum Alten Testament*, *TWOT* will nevertheless prove to be an invaluable resource tool for those engaged in, or preparing for, the ministry. Each word is arranged according to its root form, cognate terms are dealt with adequately, definitions are concise, and the usage of the word is employed to establish its meaning. Every word in Brown-Driver-Briggs is included, and each word is numerically keyed to Strong's *Exhaustive Concordance*. All things considered, *TWOT* must stand as one of the most valuable OT works produced to date. Highly recommended.　　　　　221.4'4.H24

Unger, Merrill F., and **William White, Jr.**, eds. *Nelson's Expository Dictionary of the Old Testament*. Nashville: Thomas Nelson Publishers, 1980.

A handy dictionary arranged alphabetically by English word, with the Hebrew equivalent(s) listed according to their verbal, nounal, adverbial, and adjectival forms. Theological issues are blended with etymological distinctions and word usage to make this a handy resource tool for lay people. Should be in every church library.　　　　221.4'4.N33

New Testament

*Bauer, Walter. *A Greek-English Lexicon of the New Testament and Other Early Christian Literature*. Translated and adapted from the 5th German ed. by W. F. Arndt and F. W. Gingrich. Revised by F. W. Gingrich and F. W. Danker. Chicago: University of Chicago Press, 1979.

A new edition of a standard work. Besides adding Bauer's new material, Dr. Gingrich, of Albright College, Reading, Pennsylvania, and Dr. Danker, of Christ Seminary—Seminex, St. Louis, have corrected errors in the first edition, increased references to textual variants and parallel usage, added new words, made references to Qumran and the Bodmer Papyri, and added thousands of entries to the bibliographies.　　　487.4.B32 1979

Computer-Konkordanz zum Novum Testamentum Graece. Edited by the Institut für Neutestamentliche Textforschung. Berlin, West Germany: Walter de Gruyter, 1980.

Based on the 26th edition of the Nestle-Aland *Novum Testamentum Graece* and the 3d edition of the United Bible Societies' *Greek New Testament*, this computer concordance is more complete than any of its predecessors, includes occurrences of conjunctions, participles, pericope, etc. Gives promise of becoming one of the most widely consulted Greek concordances available today. Highly recommended.　　　　　483.C73

Leon-Dufour, Xavier, ed. *Dictionary of the New Testament*. Translated by T. Prendergast. 3d ed. San Francisco: Harper and Row, 1980.

†This up-dated edition continues the many excellencies of its predecessors. Tables of money equivalencies, linear measures, a chronology of the life of the apostle Paul, etc., further enhance the usefulness of the fine work. Roman Catholic.　225.3.L55 1980

*Lightfoot, John. *A Commentary on the New Testament from the Talmud and Hebraica*. 4 vols. Grand Rapids: Baker Book House, 1979.

Preceded Strack and Billerbeck's *Kommentar zum Neuen Testament* by nearly three hundred years, yet remains the only work of its kind in English. Covers Matthew through I Corinthians and relates the teaching of the Talmud to the writings of the NT. Deserves careful study. Recommended.

225.7.L62 1979.

Meyer, Heinrich August Wilhelm. *Commentary on the New Testament*. 11 vols. Winona Lake, IN: Alpha Productions, 1979-80.

Beautifully reproduced from the 1906 edition, and with the translation carefully checked by some of the most capable scholars of the day, these volumes make available once more the rich treasures which made this work one of the most eagerly sought after at the turn of the century. In areas where this work is now dated, reference will need to be made to more recent treatments. Readers, however, should not neglect the solid evangelical scholarship which made this set justly famous.

225.7.M57

Pastoral Resources

Bartlett, John. *Familiar Quotations*. Edited by E.M. Beck. 15th ed. Boston: Little, Brown and Company, 1980.

Considerably enlarged and brought up to date, this resource work retains its well-deserved popularity.　　　808.88.B28 1980

Ehrlich, Eugene, et al., eds. and compilers. *Oxford American Dictionary*. New York: Oxford University Press, 1980.

Building upon the distinguished tradition of Oxford dictionaries, this work contains all the words one is likely to hear or read. It features American spelling, pronunciation, usage, and idioms. Emphasizes concise and precise definitions, and does not use synonyms to define words unless they distinguish shades of meaning.   423.0X2A 1980

Chapter 2

BIBLE

Study of the Bible

Calvin, John. *Commentaries*. Translated and edited by J. Haroutunian. Library of Christian Classics. Philadelphia: Westminster Press, 1979.
Selections from Calvin's commentaries on topics like the Bible, the knowledge of God, Jesus Christ, the Christian life, faith, providence, election and predestination, ethics and the common life, and the church.
220.08.C11 1979

Coleman, Lucien E., Jr. *How to Teach the Bible*. Nashville: Broadman Press, 1979.
A helpful word for use by DCEs and those involved in the training of teachers.
220'.07.C67 1979

Hromas, R. P. *Passport to the Bible*. Wheaton, IL: Tyndale House Publishers, 1980.
The author teaches Bible study groups in her home and church. In this handy book she shares with her readers the principles of personal study which she has found successful.
220'.07.H85

Lockerbie, D. Bruce. *Asking Questions: A Classroom Model for Teaching the Bible*. Milford, MI: Mott Media, 1980.

A commendable book on Bible study methodology. Analyzes the technique of asking questions used by the Lord Jesus and then applies the principles to select passages of the OT. Recommended.
220'.07.L79

Stott, John Robert Walmsey. *Understanding the Bible*. Grand Rapids: Zondervan Publishing House, 1979.
First published in England in 1972, this study guide by one of the great expository preachers of our generation answers questions new Christians are asking and shows how they may benefit from, and be nurtured by, the Word of God.
220.07.S7

Tollers, Vincent L., and **John R. Maier**, eds. *The Bible in Its Literary Milieu: Contemporary Essays*. Grand Rapids: Wm. B. Eerdmans Publishing Co., 1979.
A stimulating collection of essays by both conservative and liberal scholars, each discussing a form of literature or the contribution of some other discipline to our awareness of the meaning and message of different portions of Scripture. For the informed reader.
220.6.T57

Inspiration, Authority, Etc.

Achtemeier, Paul J. *The Inspiration of Scripture: Problems and Proposals*. Philadelphia: Westminster Press, 1980.
The author adopts a mediating stance. He refers to the works of A. A. Hodge and B. B. Warfield, but fails to interact with other evangelical writers. He does discuss the use of the Bible in the church and advocates its "authority," but not in the sense of "Thus saith the Lord."
220.13.AC4

Bavinck, Herman. *The Philosophy of Revelation*. Grand Rapids: Baker Book House, 1979.
Contains the L. P. Stone Lectures, Princeton Seminary, 1908-09. Traces the idea of revelation in its biblical form and content, and develops a view of man in relation to the creation that paves the way for an understanding of the plan and purpose of God in revelation. Reformed.
220.1.B32

Bush, L. Russ, and **Tom J. Nettles.** *Baptists and the Bible: The Baptist Doctrine of Biblical Inspiration and Religious Authority in Historical Perspective.* Chicago: Moody Press, 1980.

A singularly thorough blending of the history of the inerrancy controversy with a fine refutation of the theories which have been advanced against the orthodox, conservative position.   220.13.B96

*Carroll, Benajah Harvey. *Inspiration of the Bible.* Nashville: Thomas Nelson Publishers, 1980.

Originally published in 1930—at the height of the "Fundamentalist-Modernist Controversy"—this trenchant statement of the historic Baptist position on the inspiration of the Scriptures is not only a classic in the field, but can be read with profit by pastors and laypeople today.   220.13.C23 1980

*Geisler, Norman L., ed. *Inerrancy.* Grand Rapids: Zondervan Publishing House, 1979.

One part of a series of monographs stemming from the International Conference on Biblical Inerrancy, 1978. Chapters treat crucial aspects of the debate from an evangelical perspective.   220.13.IN3G 1979

Hodge, Archibald A., and **Benjamin B. Warfield.** *Inspiration.* Grand Rapids: Baker Book House, 1979.

Reprinted from the 1881 edition, these brief essays lay bare and defend the evangelical doctrine of the self-disclosure of God to man.
220.12.H66 1979

*Johnson, Samuel Lewis, Jr. *The Old Testament in the New: An Argument for Biblical Inspiration.* Grand Rapids: Zondervan Publishing House, 1980.

Delightful studies which ably correlate the OT Scripture with the New. Demonstrate convincingly the accuracy of the Word and the viability of the doctrine of inspiration.
220.13.J63

*MacArthur, John F. Jr. *Why Believe the Bible?* Ventura, CA: Regal Books, 1980.

Twelve chapters providing a rationale for confidence in the Bible together with an explanation of the importance of the Word of God in the life of the believer.   220'.01.M11

McDonald, Hugh Dermot. *What the Bible Teaches About the Bible.* Wheaton, IL: Tyndale House Publishers, 1979.

An able discussion of the theological issues surrounding the doctrines of revelation and inspiration. Well reasoned; communicates the teaching of Scripture in terms laypeople can understand.   220'.01.M14

Packer, James Innell. *God Has Spoken.* Downers Grove, IL: InterVarsity Press, 1979.

Published in 1965, these messages reveal what has taken place in the Christian church following the neglect of the Bible as the revelation of God to man. Concludes with "The Chicago Statement on Biblical Inerrancy."
220.12.P12

*Radmacher, Earl D., ed. *Can We Trust the Bible?* Wheaton, IL: Tyndale House Publishers, 1979.

Continues the authoritative works growing out of the International Council on Biblical Inerrancy, 1977. Stimulating.
220.1.C16 1979

Ricoeur, Paul. *Essays on Biblical Interpretation.* Edited by L. S. Mudge. Philadelphia: Fortress Press, 1980.

†These extensively documented essays advance and refine the idea of the *testimonia* of the NT and the methodology whereby they may be uncovered and understood.
220.6'01.R42

Rogers, Jack B., and **Donald K. McKim.** *The Authority and Interpretation of the Bible.* San Francisco: Harper and Row, 1979.

Rogers and McKim provide an assessment of the historic views of leading theologians from Clement to the present in an endeavor to prove that the view held by conservative evangelicals today is *not* the traditional viewpoint of the church through the ages. Does not consider the evidence of Scriptures.
220.6'09.R63

Ryrie, Charles Caldwell. *What You Should Know About Inerrancy.* Chicago: Moody Press, 1980.

This book sifts through the mass of philosophical and theological verbiage and offers a clear, concise delineation of the evidence.
220.13.R99

Sabourin, Leopold. *The Bible and Christ: The Unity of the Two Testaments.* Staten Island, NY: Alba House, 1980.

Known for his scholarship, Sabourin here turns from exegesis and exposition to bibliography and the nature of revelation. He delineates the scope of the OT covenants and the use of typology as the bridge by which to unite the teaching of the testaments.
220.6.S1

Special Topics

Adams, Jay Edward. *Marriage, Divorce and Remarriage in the Bible*. Grand Rapids: Baker Book House, 1980.
Treats fairly the problems leading to divorce and, after discussing the biblical teaching for the resolution of these difficulties, makes a plea for forgiveness, particularly on the part of the Christian community. 220.8.M35.AD1

Anderson, Bernhard W. *The Living Word of the Bible*. Philadelphia: Westminster Press, 1979.
†This collection of sermons reveals the author's unwillingness to separate the biblical narrative from history of higher critical theories; yet treats the Bible as authoritative.
220.1.AN2

*Aharoni, Yohanan. *The Land of the Bible: A Historical Geography*. Revised and enl. ed. Translated and edited by A. F. Rainey. Philadelphia: Westminster Press, 1979.
This long-awaited revision will remain *the* authoritative work in this area of biblical research for many years to come. It deserves careful and repeated reading.
220.91.AH1 1979

Armerding, George D. *The Fragance of the Lord: Toward a Deeper Appreciation of the Bible*. New York: Harper and Row, 1979
Gleans devotional lessons from passages in which "odors" (sweet fragrance) of the Bible are mentioned. 220.8.0D5.AR5

*Baron, David. *Rays of Messiah's Glory: Christ in the Old Testament*. Winona Lake, IN: Alpha Publications, n.d.
This reprint makes available again the delightful exposition of select OT passages relating to Christ and His ministry.
220.8.B26

*Baxter, Batsell Barrett, and **Harold Hazelip**. *A Devotional Guide to Biblical Lands*. Grand Rapids: Baker Book House, 1979.
One of the best guide books ever produced.
913.3.B33

Custance, Arthur C. *The Flood: Local or Global?* Vol. 9. The Doorway Papers. Grand Rapids: Zondervan Publishing House, 1979.
Considers the fall of Adam and Eve, theodicy, and prayer, in addition to discussing the extent of the flood. Always stimulating, Custance's writings abound with preaching ideas and apologetic values. The book con-

cludes with a section on "Christian Scholarship: A Protest and a Plea."
220.8.M31.C96 v.9

_____. *Indexes of the Doorway Papers*. Vol. 10. Grand Rapids: Zondervan Publishing House, 1980.
Comprehensive index to the author's famous essays, complete with a listing of all papers; diagrams, figures, maps, and tables; subject, name, and Scripture indexes; and a listing of the discussion of Hebrew and Greek words. This volume should not be neglected, as it provides easy access to a lifetime of research. Of apologetic value.
220.8.M31.C96 v.10

_____. *The Mysterious Matter of Mind, With a Response by Lee Edward Travis*. Grand Rapids: Zondervan Publishing House, 1980.
Another important monograph on the origin and nature of the mind. Underscores the psychology of human worth, the philosophy of human life, and the practicability of each person's potential. 128.2.C96

*_____. *The Seed of the Woman*. Brockville, Ontario, Canada: Doorway Publications, 1980.
The author who gave the Christian world the inestimably rich "Doorway Papers" (Zondervan) here makes available another massive treatise in which he discusses such topics as the longevity of those living before the flood, the nature of the "forbidden fruit," the promise of God to Eve, and how the Word became flesh. Well researched, this volume is an able synthesis of the Bible with anthropology, physiology, and theology.
220.8.W84.C96

Donovan, Peter. *Interpreting Religious Experience*. New York: Seabury Press, 1979.
†Follows in the wake of the relational revolution and, by setting aside the teaching of Scripture, seeks to find validity in religious experiences. Then, after formulating philosophic principles based on these experiences, seeks to validate the conclusions reached either by an appeal to Scripture or quotations from a variety of theologians. 200'.1.D71

Ellison, Henry Leopold. *From Babylon to Bethlehem: The People of God from the Exile to the Messiah*. Atlanta: John Knox Press, 1979.
First published in England in 1976, this

important monograph treats the events of the Jews from the Babylonian captivity, through the intertestamental period, to the coming of Christ. An excellent treatment of the ministries of Nehemiah and Ezra further enhances the usefulness of the brief book. Genealogical tables are included.   933.EL5

*Fairbairn, Patrick. *The Revelation of Law in Scripture*. Winona Lake, IN: Alpha Publications, 1979.
First published in 1869, these lectures treat the moral law implanted in the heart of man and trace its use throughout the Bible. Complete with supplementary dissertations. Excellent. Reformed.   220.8.L41.F15 1979

*Feinberg, Charles Lee. *Israel at the Center of History and Revelation*. Portland, OR: Multnomah Press, 1980.
This revised edition of *Israel in the Spotlight* brings up to date the author's earlier treatise dealing with God's plan and purpose for His chosen people—past, present, and future. Recommended.   220.15.F32 1980.

Finegan, Jack. *Archaeological History of the Ancient Middle East*. Boulder, CO: Westview Press, 1979.
An indispensable, connected account of events which transpired around the Mediterranean and throughout the Fertile Crescent from circa 10,000 B.C. to 330 B.C. Illustrated. An essential reference work.   913.031.M46.F49

Foh, Susan T. *Women and the Word of God: A Response to Biblical Feminism*. Phillipsburg, NJ: Presbyterian and Reformed Publishing Co., 1980.
This discussion of feminism treats fairly the difficult issues and grapples realistically with the hard problems. The teaching of Scripture is referred to frequently and the nitty-gritty issue of submission is discussed in light of the evident androgeny within the Godhead and the willing subordination of members of the Godhead to one another.   220.8.W84.F

Hals, Ronald M. *Grace and Faith in the Old Testament*. Minneapolis: Augsburg Publishing House, 1980.
A judicious discussion which leads the author to conclude that "the basic shape in which we encounter grace and faith in both testaments is the same."   221.8.G75.H16

*Kitchen, Kenneth Anderson. *The Bible in Its World: The Bible and Archaeology Today*. Downers Grove, IL: InterVarsity Press, 1978.

A fascinating portrayal of the significance of recent archaeological discoveries for the study of the Bible. Up-to-date. A most important volume.   220.93.K64

Robinson, Henry Wheeler. *Corporate Personality in Ancient Israel*. Revised ed. Philadelphia: Fortress Press, 1980.
†First published in 1937 under the title *The Group and the Individual in Israel*, this book constructs a theological foundation for understanding personality in the OT, and considers how each Israelite contributed to the complexion of the family, tribe, and nation.   301.29'33.R56 1980

Ryrie, Charles Caldwell. *The Best Is Yet to Come*. Chicago: Moody Press, 1980.
In thirteen moving chapters Ryrie covers prophetic themes relating to the future. In each chapter he treats a new facet of eschatology and offers hope in the midst of doubt and uncertainty.   220.15.R99B

Smart, James D. *The Past, Present, and Future of Biblical Theology*. Philadelphia: Westminster Press, 1979.
†Continues the discussion begun by Childs in *Biblical Theology in Crisis*. Points to the continued resurgence of interest in biblical theology and charts a course for the future.   220.823.SM2

*Westcott, Brooke Foss. *The Bible in the Church: A Popular Account of the Collection and Reception of the Holy Scriptures in the Christian Churches*. Grand Rapids: Baker Book House, 1979.
Growing out of Westcott's excellent *History of the Canon of the New Testament*, these chapters treat relevantly and practically the reception of the biblical writings by the Church. Historically reliable. Evangelical. Deserves careful reading, particularly by those who are troubled by denials of inspiration, authority, and canonicity. Recommended.   220.52'09.W52 1979

White, Reginald Ernest Oscar. *Biblical Ethics*. Grand Rapids: Wm. B. Eerdmans Publishing Co., 1979.
A learned, but disappointing, work. The author grounds his teaching upon the Scriptures, but only after he has interpreted them in the light of the latest *Form-* and *Redactiongeschichte*.   220.817.W58

Chapter 3

OLD TESTAMENT

Special Studies

Anderson, G. W., ed. *Tradition and Interpretation: Essays by Members of the Society for Old Testament Study.* Oxford: Clarendon Press, 1979.

Continues the series begun by A. S. Peake in *The People and the Book* (1925). Contains thirteen essays on different problem areas of the OT, from Pentateuchal criticism to apocalyptic literature.   221'.06.T67

Becker, Joachim. *Messianic Expectation in the Old Testament.* Translated by David E. Green. Edinburgh: T. and T. Clark, 1980.

Based upon the historical-critical interpretation of the OT, these chapters scrutinize some key passages and then succinctly relate the essence of their teaching to the NT.
221.8.M56.B38

Bernstein, Burton. *Sinai: The Great and Terrible Wilderness.* New York: Viking Press, 1979.

Based on personal visits to the isolated, yet strategic, peninsula, Bernstein recreates Israel's past while also providing his readers with an understanding of the present. A blending of historical, social, and cultural facts into a single narrative. Interesting reading.
953'.1.B45

Blanch, Stuart. *The Trumpet in the Morning: Law and Freedom Today in the Light of the Hebraeo-Christian Tradition.* New York: Oxford University Press, 1979.

†Containing the Chavasse Lectures for 1977, each chapter treats with theological acumen and practical relevance some aspect of the OT law and its application to the present. Stimulating.   221.8.L41.B59

Childs, Brevard S. *Introduction to the Old Testament as Scripture.* Philadelphia: Fortress Press, 1979.

Not since Harrison's *Introduction to the*

Old Testament has anything as comprehensive as this been attempted. Based upon form-critical theories, this scholarly study exhibits the very best that liberal theological scholarship has to offer.   221.6.C43

Delitzsch, Franz Julius. *Old Testament History of Redemption.* Translated by S. I. Curtiss. Winona Lake, IN: Alpha Publications, 1980.

Containing lectures delivered in Leipzig in 1880, this companion volume to the author's *Messianic Prophecies* follows the history of God's progressive revelation and explains the development of the doctrine of salvation in the OT.   221.8.S3.D37

Dryness, William. *Themes in Old Testament Theology.* Downers Grove, IL: Inter-Varsity Press, 1979.

Provocative studies of the revelation and nature of God, creation and providence, man and woman, sin, the covenant and the law, and other themes. Missing is a development of the theocracy and the grounding of ethics in the "fear of the Lord." Enlightening and rewarding reading.   221.8'23.D84

Green, William Henry. *General Introduction to the Old Testament: The Canon.* Grand Rapids: Baker Book House, 1980.

First published in 1898, this discussion of God's progressive revelation tests the prevailing theories of canonicity and provides a convincing answer to the following questions: When was the canon completed? What books were included? and How were people made aware of the uniqueness of sacred Scripture? Advocates a three-fold division of the canon.
221.12.G82 1980

Ishida, Tomoo. *The Royal Dynasties in Ancient Israel: A Study on the Formation and Development of Royal-Dynastic Ideology.*

Berlin: Walter de Gruyter, 1977.

†A scholarly discussion of the monarchies of the ancient Near East, particularly the Davidic dynasty, but stops short of carrying the OT teaching into the New and showing how Christ will fulfill all that the OT foreshadowed in type and prophecy.

221.8.K61.IS3

*Kurtz, Johann Heinrich. *Sacrificial Worship in the Old Testament.* Translated by J. Martin. Minneapolis: Klock and Klock Christian Publishers, 1980.

A work of genius which grasps the significance of the Levitical system of sacrifices and explains their symbolism in relation to the forgiveness of sins. However, as is explained in the foreword, Kurtz fails to treat Israel's worship in light of the theocracy and does not lay a foundation for the development of the priesthood of all believers in the NT. Commendable, in spite of these weaknesses.

221.8.S11.K96

Littauer, M. A., and J. H. Crouwel. *Wheeled Vehicles and Ridden Animals in the Ancient Near East.* Leiden, The Netherlands: E. J. Brill, 1979.

A historical survey of vehicles for conveyance—domestic, economic, and military—from the first to the third millennium B.C. Well researched. Highlights the use of animals in the OT, particularly in warfare.

221.8.T68.L71

Neil, William. *Can We Trust the Old Testament.* New York: Seabury Press, 1979.

Intended as a companion volume to J. Robinson's *Can We Trust the New Testament.* Adheres to the major tenets of modern critical scholarship. While well written, this work fails to treat seriously the traditional view of the inspiration of the Scripture held by the conservative evangelical wing of the church. Disappointing.   221.12.N31

Rad, Gerhard von. *God at Work in Israel.* Translated by John H. Marks. Nashville: Abingdon Press, 1980.

First published in German in 1974, this series of lectures/essays covers a variety of OT themes, from "How to Read the OT" to concepts of life and death. It includes some character studies and a few critical chapters on Mosaic monotheism, creation, etc. Adheres throughout to theories of higher criticism.

221.8.R11

*Raven, John Howard. *The History of the Religion of Israel: An Old Testament Theology.* Grand Rapids: Baker Book House, 1979.

Written by one of the great conservative theologians of the past, this work was first published privately in 1933. It contains a fine delineation of OT theology from the time of Moses to Manasseh. Makes an outstanding contribution. Reformed.   221.82.R19 1979

Rogerson, J. W. *Anthropology and the Old Testament.* Atlanta: John Knox Press, 1979.

A careful discussion of the OT teaching on the nature of man. Well researched, but impaired by the author's adherence to theologically liberal tenets.

221.8.M31.R63 (Alt.DDC 223).

*Schultz, Samuel J. *The Old Testament Speaks.* 3d ed. San Francisco: Harper and Row, 1980.

Having served the needs of collegians for twenty years, this work, in its revised edition, continues to be one of the ablest of conservative historical introductions to the OT.

221.61.SCH8 1980.

Whitelam, Keith W. *The Just King: Monarchical Judicial Authority in Ancient Israel.* Sheffield, England: University of Sheffield Press, 1979.

Based on the author's dissertation at the University of Manchester, this partial treatment of the Davidic dynasty and the continuation of the theocracy through David's line, makes a distinct contribution to the anticipation of the Messiah and the establishment of His kingdom. Of great value to students of Bible history.   222.44'06.W58

*Wood, Leon J. *Israel's United Monarchy.* Grand Rapids: Baker Book House, 1979.

A refreshing excursus into Israel's history, the dawn of the "Golden Age," and the strengths and weaknesses of the first three kings. Excellent.   222.43'09.W85 1979

Würthwein, Ernst. *The Text of the Old Testament: An Introduction to the Biblia Hebraica.* Translated by E. F. Rhodes. Grand Rapids: Wm. B. Eerdmans Publishing Co., 1979.

Based upon the 4th German edition (1973), this work is of the utmost value to the student of the OT. It surveys the transmission of the text and includes pertinent historical and philological comments on the MT, Samaritan Pentateuch, the different Targums, the Syriac version, etc. A valuable introduction.

221.4.W95 1979.

Historical Books

*Adeney, Walter Frederick. *Ezra and Nehemiah*. Minneapolis: Klock and Klock Christian Publishers, 1980.
One of the best works on this facet of Israel's post-exilic history. Can be read with profit by both pastor and layperson.
222.7.AD3 1980

*Alford, Henry. *The Book of Genesis, and Part of the Book of Exodus*. Minneapolis: Klock and Klock Christian Publishers, 1979.
While accepting a modified form of the Documentary Hypothesis, Alford succeeds in bringing to his study of the OT the same depth of insight and richness of thought that characterized his treatment of the NT. A rare work; buy it while it is available.
222.11'07.AL2 1979

Bonar, Horatius. *Thoughts on Genesis*. Grand Rapids: Kregel Publishers, 1979.
First published in 1875 under the title *Earth's Morning*, these devotional studies of Genesis 1–6, covering the period from Adam to the flood, are permeated with practical application of biblical truth to life.
222.11'06.B64 1–6 1979.

Candlish, Robert Smith. *Studies in Genesis*. Grand Rapids: Kregel Publications, 1979.
First published in 1868, this is one of *the* great expositions on Genesis. Highlights the doctrinal issues and biographical features. A fine example of expository preaching.
222.11'06.C16 1979.

Clines, David J. A. *The Theme of the Pentateuch*. Sheffield, England: University of Sheffield Press, 1978.
Advocates the unity of the Pentateuch in its original form; challenges the two major tendencies in OT research, atomism and geneticism. Advocates an approach to the Mosaic writings which is encouraging to see. Recommended.
222.1'06.C61

Davidson, Robert. *Genesis 12–50*. Cambridge Bible Commentary on the New English Bible. Cambridge: Cambridge University Press, 1979.
If one makes allowance for redaction and adherence to documentary sources, Davidson's work has some value due for historical references and occasional exegetical insights.
222.11'07.D28 12–50.

Davies, G. I. *The Way of the Wilderness: A Geographical Study of the Wilderness Itineraries in the Old Testament*. Cambridge: Cambridge University Press, 1979.
Focuses on the Exodus, evaluates the possible routes the Israelites might have taken, and traces the development of the Exodus motif in Jewish, Christian, and Arabic writings.
222.12'095.D28W

*Davis, John D. *Genesis and Semitic Tradition*. Grand Rapids: Baker Book House, 1980.
First published in 1894, this conservative work by a Reformed Bible scholar demonstrates the uniqueness and integrity of the OT when compared with literary material from the ancient Near East. Most valuable.
222.11'06.D29 1980

*Davis, John James and John Clement Whitcomb, Jr. *A History of Israel from Conquest to Exile*. Grand Rapids: Baker Book House, 1980.
A compilation of books covering Israel's history from the period of Joshua and the Judges to the Babylonian exile. Valuable for its adherence to the text and the correlation of geographical, literary, and political source material with the biblical narrative.
221.95.D29 1980.

Flynn, Leslie B. *Joseph: God's Man in Egypt*. Wheaton, IL: Victor Books. 1979.
Brief, inspirational messages designed for adult discussion groups.
221.92.J77.F67

*Green, William Henry. *The Unity of the Book of Genesis*. Grand Rapids: Baker Book House, 1979.
First published in 1895, this volume answers the adherents of the Documentary Hypothesis point-by-point. Green maintains the consistency, harmony, unity, and Mosaic authorship of Genesis, and succeeds in demolishing higher critical theories. We welcome the reappearance of this long-neglected work.
222.11'07.G82 1979.

Gunn, David M. *The Story of King David: Genre and Interpretation*. Sheffield, England: University of Sheffield Press, 1978.
Well researched and indexed, this assessment of David's service as king of Israel provides new and important insights into the history of the times, the literary mold in which the narrative is cast, and the private and

political milieu in which David lived and moved.   221.92.D28.G95

*Harrison, Roland Kenneth. *Leviticus, an Introduction and Commentary.* Tyndale Old Testament Commentaries. Downers Grove, IL: InterVarsity Press. 1980.
A fitting introduction to the regulations and rituals, sacrifices and offerings of the Levitical code. Does not evade interpretative problems and provides a firm basis for the understanding of NT teaching of the atonement of Christ and the priesthood of believers.
222.13'07.H24

Huffman, John A., Jr. *Liberating Limits: A Fresh Look at the Ten Commandments.* Waco, TX: Word Books, 1980.
Not since Joy Davidman's *Smoke on the Mountain* has a work as interesting and relevant as this one been published. Huffman treats the Decalogue as the sage counsel of God the Father to His children to "protect" them from their own destructive tendencies.
222.16.H87

Hyatt, James Philip. *Exodus.* New Century Bible Commentary. Grand Rapids: Wm. B. Eerdmans Publishing Co., 1980.
Manifests little regard for the integrity of the MT. Reconstructs the history and theology of this era of Israel's history after adopting a late date for the Exodus. First published in 1972.   222.12'07. 1980

Julien, Tom. *Spiritual Greatness—Studies in Exodus.* Winona Lake, IN: BMH Books, 1979.
Clear concise, well-outlined studies. Useful for adult study groups.
222.12'07.J94

Kidner, Derek. *Ezra and Nehemiah, An Introduction and Commentary.* Tyndale Old Testament Commentaries. Downers Grove, IL: InterVarsity Press, 1979.
All that readers of the author's other expository studies have come to expect is to be found in this timely study of Ezra-Nehemiah. It is to be regretted, however, that Kidner follows the highly critical view of the size of Nehemiah's Jerusalem, has only a brief treatment of chap. 3, and devotes only a page and a half to chap. 7. In spite of these weaknesses, his comments are judicious.
222.7'07.K54

Lewis, Arthur H. *Judges/Ruth.* Chicago: Moody Press, 1979.
A contemporary reflection on the relevancy of these OT books. Valuable for adult study groups.   222.3'07.L58

McCarther, P. Kyle, Jr. *The Anchor Bible: I Samuel, a New Translation with Introduction, Notes and Commentary.* Garden City, NY: Doubleday and Company, 1980.
†Attempts numerous reconstructions of the MT, yet is instructive and up-to-date.
222.43'07.M11

*Murphy, James Gracey. *A Critical and Exegetical Commentary on the Book of Exodus.* Minneapolis: Klock and Klock Christian Publishers, 1980.
Easily ranks with the best works produced on Exodus and, for the general reader, may be placed higher. A learned, judicious, and reverent treatment.   222.12'07.M95

*Raleigh, Alexander. *Book of Esther: Its Practical Lessons and Dramatic Scenes.* Minneapolis: Klock and Klock Christian Publishers, 1980.
A refreshing study based upon a literal interpretation of the text. Each character is analyzed with "insight approaching genius," and the practical application of Scripture is accomplished with rare skill.
222.9'07.R13 1980

Sasson, Jack M. *Ruth: A New Translation with a Philological Commentary and a Formalist-Folklorist Interpretation.* Baltimore: Johns Hopkins University Press, 1979.
†Photoduplicated from typed pages, this technical commentary provides some valuable insights into the text, but is disappointing in its interpretation of the theme and purpose of this short book.   222'.35'07.S7

Wenham, Gordon J. *The Book of Leviticus.* New International Commentary on the Old Testament. Grand Rapids: Wm. B. Eerdmans Publishing Co., 1979.
Following a brief introduction and a selective bibliography containing all the best books and journal articles, Wenham settles down to expound the text. Each section is prefaced by a translation of the MT. Following an historical assessment of the teaching of the passage, "the abiding theological value" of the passage is discussed. The result is a valuable contribution to the biblical preacher's library.
222.13'07.W48

*Whitcomb, John Clement, Jr. *Esther: The Triumph of God's Sovereignty.* Chicago: Moody Press, 1979.
Intended for lay people, this devout commentary deals judiciously with the text and relates the history of the times to the Biblical narrative. Excellent.   222.9'07.W58

Poetical Books

*Bridges, Charles. *A Modern Study in the Book of Proverbs: Charles Bridges' Classic Revised for Today's Reader by George F. Santa*. Milford, MI: Mott Media, 1978.

Rewritten in modern English, using the text of the NASB, carefully cross-indexed, and accompanied by a valuable topical index, this modern reissue of Bridges' indispensable work should prove stimulating to contemporary Bible students.   223.7'07.B76 1978

Bullock, C. Hassell. *An Introduction to the Poetic Books of the Old Testament (The Wisdom and Songs of Israel)*. Chicago: Moody Press, 1979.

A thorough, well-written introduction to the poetic writings of the OT. Includes a section on the theology of wisdom literature. Will be used repeatedly by teachers in Bible colleges and seminaries. Recommended. 223'.06.B87

Clarke, Arthur G. *Analytical Studies in the Psalms*. Grand Rapids: Kregel Publishers, 1979.

Written during his imprisonment by the Japanese in North China during World War I, these brief analyses of each psalm breathe the confidence of one whose reliance is established upon the unchanging character of God. Ideal for use in a series of expository studies.   223.2'06.C55 1979

Dickson, David. *A Commentary on the Psalms*. 2 vols. Minneapolis: Klock and Klock Christian publishers, 1980.

First published in 1655, these devout studies of ancient Israel's hymnic literature exhibit a vibrancy of faith and a care in expounding the text that is refreshing. Reformed.
223.2'07.D56 1980

Loader, J. A. *Polar Structures in the Book of Qohlet*. Berlin: Walter de Gruyter, 1979.

Analyzes the polar structures of Ecclesiastes and uses these to highlight the tensions created in the experience of the author. For the well-informed student.
223.8'062.L78

Rowley, Harold Henry. *Job*. New Century Bible Commentary. Grand Rapids: Wm. B. Eerdmans Publishing Co., 1980.

First published in 1970, this study is not a commentary in the strict sense of the word, but treats specific words or phrases in different verses. Insightful.   223.1'07.R79 1980

Santa, George F. *Proverbs: Personalized Studies for Practical Living; for Use with a Modern Study in the Book of Proverbs*. Milford, MI: Mott Media, 1978.

A topical summary of the contents of Proverbs with hints on how to study this much-neglected portion of God's Word.
223.4'06.S5

Westermann, Claus. *The Psalms: Structure, Content and Message*. Translated by Ralph D. Gehrke. Minneapolis: Augsburg Publishing House, 1980.

†Discusses different types of hymnic literature, and seeks to relate the message of the Psalms to life today.   223.2'06.W52

Prophetic Books

Andersen, Francis Ian, and David Noel Freedman. *The Anchor Bible: Hosea, a New Translation with Introduction and Commentary*. Garden City, NY: Doubleday and Company, 1980.

A complete and thorough explanation of the prophet's message with a fascinating interpretation of his life and work. Can be read with profit even by those who would have preferred a more accurate presentation of the eschatological aspects of the OT book.
224.7'07.AN3

Clements, Ronald Ernest. *Isaiah 1–39*. New Century Bible Commentary. Grand Rapids: Wm. B. Eerdmans Publishing Co., 1980.

Treats the text with rare insight and provides readers, if not with a commentary, at least with scholarly comments on selected words and phrases.224.1'07.C59 1980

Coote, Robert B. *Amos Among the Prophets: Composition and Theology*. Philadelphia: Fortress Press, 1981.

Coote makes provision for three stages of

composition before beginning to analyze the content and assess the theological importance of this OT prophecy.   224.9'06.C78

Culver, Robert Duncan. *The Histories and Prophecies of Daniel.* Winona Lake, IN: BMH Books, 1980.
A fact-filled, biblically-based exposition which explains the meaning and message of Daniel's prophecy. An ideal work for home Bible classes and adult Sunday school groups.
224.5'07.C89

Efird, James M. *Jeremiah: Prophet Under Siege.* Valley Forge, PA: Judson Press, 1979.
Designed for use by lay people, this topical approach to the life of Jeremiah treats only incidentally the arrangement of the book and the prophet's messages.   224.2'06.EF4

*****Fairbairn, Patrick.** *An Exposition of Ezekiel.* Minneapolis: Klock and Klock Christian Publishers, 1979.
Makes judicious use of the Hebrew text, but not at the expense of the English reader. Provides a timely exposition which is devotional as well as historical and practical. Recommended. Amillenial.
224.4'07.F15 1979

Ford, Desmond. *Daniel.* Nashville: Southern Publishing Association, 1978.
Employs the text of the RSV. Expounds the text with insight and an awareness of the history of the ancient Near East as well as the political machinations and their prophetic implications. Poorly bound.   224.5'07.F75

*****Hindson, Edward E.** *Isaiah's Immanuel: A Sign of His Times, Or the Sign of the Ages?* Grand Rapids: Baker Book House, 1978.
In no way duplicates the material covered by Lawlor in *Almah . . . Virgin or Young Woman*, or Gromachi in *The Virgin Birth*. Treats cogently and well the difficulties of Isaiah 7 and applies the teaching of the text in the best evangelical tradition.   232.1.H58

*****Kelly, William.** *An Exposition of the Book of Isaiah.* 4th ed. Minneapolis: Klock and Klock Christian Publishers, 1979.
Fills a long-standing need for a premillennial commentary by a well-informed writer. Recommended to readers of the English text.
224.1'07.K28 1979

*****Tatford, Frederick Albert.** *Daniel and His Prophecy: Studies in the Prophecy of Daniel.* Minneapolis: Klock and Klock Christian Publishers, 1980.
First published in 1953, this study exhibits a balance between extremes. It treats the prophetic word with respect, but does not probe minutiae. Instead, the Biblical text is expounded for the edification and enlightenment of the believer. Included is a masterful blending of history and theology, practical application and devotional stimulation. Premillennial.   224.5'07.T18

*****Thompson, John Arthur.** *The Book of Jeremiah.* New International Commentary on the Old Testament. Grand Rapids: Wm. B. Eerdmans Publishing Co., 1980.
This highly competent commentary deals thoroughly with every aspect of the prophet's life and ministry, and stresses the importance of Judah's covenant relationship with the Lord. Readers here are treated to a careful handling of the Hebrew text ably correlated with the DSS, and a definitive handling of the Josianic reformation. Recommended.
224.2'07.T37

*****Wright, Charles Henry Hamilton.** *Zechariah and His Prophecies, Considered in Relation to Modern Criticism.* Minneapolis: Klock and Klock Christian Publishers, 1980.
Comprising the author's Bampton Lextures at Oxford University, 1878, these extensive studies translate, introduce, and treat the visions of this neglected OT prophet. Amillenial.   224.98'07.W93

Chapter 4

NEW TESTAMENT

Texts, and Grammatical and Textual Studies

Aland, Kurt, et al., eds. *The Greek New Testament*. 3d ed. New York: United Bible Societies, 1977.
With a new preface and a completely revised textual apparatus, this latest edition should be a constant source of delight to users.
225.48.G81 1977.

Burgon, John William. *The Revision Revised*. Paradise, PA: Conservative Classics, 1979.
Long out of print, this classic by the renowned Dean of Chichester was first published in 1883. In this work, Burgon takes issue with Westcott and Hort and advocates the acceptance of the Textus Receptus.
225.4.B91 1979

Carson, D. A. *The King James Version Debate: A Plea for Realism*. Grand Rapids: Baker Book House, 1979.
A powerful polemic in favor of modern translations of the Bible coupled with an equally powerful analysis and repudiation of Pickering's *The Identity of the New Testament Text*.
225.4.C23

Chamberlain, William Douglas. *An Exegetical Grammar of the Greek New Testament*. Grand Rapids: Baker Book House, 1979.
First published in 1941, this introductory work has been widely used in Bible colleges and seminaries. Comprehensive and helpful.
485.C35 1979

Deissmann, Gustav Adolf. *Bible Studies*. Translated by A. Grieve. Winona Lake, IN: Alpha Publications, 1979.
First published in English in 1901, this companion volume to the author's famous *Light From the Ancient East* relates the usage of specific words found in papryi fragments and on inscriptions to the text of the NT.
225.848.D36B 1979

Estrada, David, and William White. *The First New Testament*. Nashville: Thomas Nelson Publishers, 1978.
Elaborates upon the proposal made by Fr. Jose O'Callahan of Barcelona, that Fragment 5 from Qumran and other fragments from the same came from Mark's Gospel and other NT books. Contains photographs, drawings, and inscriptions of fragments.
225.48.ES8

*Hort, Fenton John Anthony**, and **Arthur Fenton Hart.** *Expository and Exegetical Studies: Compendium of Works Formerly Published Separately*. Minneapolis: Klock and Klock Christian Publishers, 1980.
Includes the hard-to-obtain exegetical and expository studies of Hort and notes on the Greek text of Mark's gospel by Hort's son.
225.'06.H78 1980.

Lightfoot, Joseph Barber. *Biblical Essays*. Grand Rapids: Baker Book House, 1979.
A series of brilliant, devout essays on John's Gospel, the preparation of Paul for the ministry, the churches Paul founded in Macedonia, the structure of Romans, etc. Indispensable.
225.8.L62

Mare, W. Harold. *Mastering New Testament Greek*. Grand Rapids: Baker Book House, 1979.
Designed as a "beginning Greek grammar" with "lesson plans for intermediate and advanced Greek students," this able treatment will undoubtedly become a standard introductory text in many colleges and seminaries.
487.5.M33

Nestle, E., and E. Nestle. *Novum Testament Graece*. Edited by K. Aland *et al.* 26th ed. Stuttgart, Germany: Deutsche Bibelstiftung, 1979.
Containing a completely reset text, with the

latest manuscript evidence in the footnotes, this work represents the latest consensus of modern NT scholars. Also of considerable interest are the new introduction and especially the editors' comments relating to the discarding of symbols for the Hesychian and Koinē texts, and the inclusion of *M*, signifying the "Majority text." 225.48.N85 1979

The New King James Bible New Testament. Nashville: Thomas Nelson and Son, 1979.
A revision of the AV of the NT. Brings the 1611 version into conformity with twentieth-century English usage. 225.52.N42

*Rienecher, Fritz. *A Linguistic Key to the Greek New Testament*. Vol. 2: *Romans– Revelation*. Translated, with additions and revisions, by Cleon L. Rogers, Jr. Grand Rapids: Zondervan Publishing House, 1980.

Long awaited, this volume completes in English the eminently usable *Sprachlichen Schuessel zum Griechischen Neuen Testament*. Makes available a vast resource of material relating to the grammar of the NT. Parsing, as well as hints about possible translation, is included. Every pastor should keep this work on his desk and refer to it each time he preaches from the NT. 225.48.R44R v.2

*Turner, Nigel. *Christian Words*. Edinburgh: T. and T. Clark, 1980.
Delves into the fascinating world of lexical studies and discovers in the usage of some NT words a significance and meaning often passed over in those works which ignore the contribution of Jewish intertestamental studies to the understanding of the NT.
225.848.T85

Hermeneutical Studies

Cartlidge, David R., and David L. Dungan. *Documents for the Study of the Gospels*. Philadelphia: Fortress Press, 1980.
Provides, in handy format, translations of Gnostic texts relating to the birth, life, and ministry of Jesus. Details Greek, Jewish and Roman thought paralleling the milieu of the Gospels. 226'.06.C24

Kistemaker, Simon J. *The Gospels in Current Study*. 2d ed. Grand Rapids: Baker Book House, 1980.
First published in 1972, this important volume provides brief pointed evangelical responses to the claims of radical critics who have frequently failed to find their erroneous theories rebutted by a theologically competent NT scholar. Kistemaker provides such a rebuttal. 226'.06.K64 1980

Mays, James Luther, ed. *Interpreting the Gospels*. Philadelphia: Fortress Press, 1981.
†In twenty scholarly chapters, taken from the pages of *Interpretation*, contributors deal with thorny problems in hermeneutics, ranging from Paul's view of the gospel to Johannine eschatology. This book is of value to seminarians for interaction and discussion.
225.6.IN8M

Simcox, William Henry. *The Language of the New Testament*. Winona Lake, IN: Alpha Publication, 1980.
A clear, concise introduction to the grammar of the Greek NT. Recommended for beginners. 487.5.S4

*Thiselton, Anthony C. *The Two Horizons: New Testament Hermeneutics and Philosophical Description with Special Reference to Heidegger, Bultmann, Gadamer, and Wittgenstein*. Grand Rapids: Wm. B. Eerdmans Publishing Co., 1980.
†Admirably fulfills the subtitle and provides a masterly introduction to the science of hermeneutics. 225.6'01.T34

Special Studies

*Bruce, Alexander Balmain. *The Miracles of Christ*. Minneapolis: Klock and Klock Christian Publishers, 1980.
Vindicates a belief in miracles in the face of the most plausible unbelief. Valuable as a work on apologetics. Will richly reward the discerning reader. 226.7'06.B83 1980.

*———. *The Parables of Christ*. Minneapolis: Klock and Klock Christian Publishers, 1980.
A fresh study of the parables which readily dispenses with the older approaches and establishes new parameters for modern research. Stimulating. 226.8'06.B83 1980.

Hagner, Donald A., and **Murray J. Harris**, eds. *Pauline Studies: Essays Presented to Professor F. F. Bruce on his 70th Birthday.* Grand Rapids: Wm. B. Eerdmans Publishing Co., 1980.

A second *Festschrift* honoring the contribution of Prof. Bruce. Part I deals with the life and theology of the Apostle Paul, and Part II focuses on literary and exegetical aspects of the Pauline writings. 225.9'24.B83.H12

Hill, David. *New Testament Prophecy.* Atlanta: John Knox Press, 1979.

Of value for its historic treatment of Jewish apocalyptic literature. Hill bases his assessment of NT Prophecy on *Redactionge-schichte*, but fails to develop a consistent view of eschatology which will adequately integrate all the evidence. 225.8.P94.M55

Kissinger, Warren S. *The Parables of Jesus: A History of Interpretation and Bibliography.* Metuchen, NJ: Scarecrow Press, 1979.

Begins with a delineation of the chief exponents of the parables from Irenaeus through Dodd to Crossan; then provides a comprehensive bibliography on each parable. Most helpful. Indexed. 226.8'06.K64

Kistemaker, Simon J. *The Parables of Jesus.* Grand Rapids: Baker Book House, 1980.

Written to aid pastors in the preparation of sermons on the parables, Kistemaker gives evidence of careful research. Ably illustrates the biblical material from extra-biblical sources (*e.g.*, Dead Sea Scrolls, Gnostic materials, etc.). Thorough. 226.8.K64

*****Ramsey, William Mitchell.** *The Historical Geography of Asia Minor.* New York: Cooper Square Publishers, 1972.

Though dated, this outstanding classic has long been out of print. It describes the composition of the peoples of ancient Asia Minor, the geographic divisions of the land, and the bishoprics established as Christianity took root. Still valuable. 225.91.R14 1972

Sampley, J. Paul. *Pauline Partnership in Christ: Christian Community and Commitment in Light of Roman Law.* Philadelphia: Fortress Press, 1980.

This vigorous, scholarly discussion of the mission of the church blends history and sociology with an exegetical explanation of selected passages from the Pauline corpus. Gives evidence of much originality of thought. 262.S4

Simcox, William Henry. *The Writers of the New Testament, Their Style and Characteristics.* Winona Lake, IN: Alpha Publications, 1980.

A remarkably perceptive introduction to the literary style of the writers of the NT. While brief, it abounds with important insights. Well indexed. 225.6.S4 1980

Stephens, Shirley. *A New Testament View of Women.* Nashville: Broadman Press, 1980.

Avoids the rabid extremes of "Women's Lib" and the inflexibility of traditionalism, and in their place offers a balanced statement of the biblical evidence. 225.8.W84.S4

*****Westcott, Brooke Foss.** *A General Survey of the History of the Canon of the New Testament.* Grand Rapids: Baker Book House, 1980.

After more than a century, this work remains the definitive treatment on the canonicity of the NT Scriptures. 225.12.W52 1980

*****Yamauchi, Edwin M.** *The Archaeology of New Testament Cities in Western Asia Minor.* Grand Rapids: Baker Book House, 1980.

Popularly written, this handy volume seeks to anchor a preacher's messages in the NT documents and the history and literature of the Graeco-Roman world. Deals with the geography and culture of the cities of Revelation 2–3 as well as several other important commercial centers. Excellent. 225.93.Y1

The Gospels and Acts

*****Alexander, Joseph Addison.** *Commentary on the Gospel of Mark.* Minneapolis: Klock and Klock Christian Publishers, 1980.

Still worthy of the busy pastor's time and attention in spite of the passage of years. 226.3'07.AL2 1980

*_____. *Commentary on the Acts of the*

Apostles. 2 vols. in 1. Minneapolis: Klock and Klock Christian Publishers, 1980.

A beautifully produced work which brings within the reach of the busy pastor the benefits of this commentator's prodigious labor. 226.6'07.AL2 1980

*_____. *The Gospel According to Mat-*

thew. Lynchburg, VA: James Family Publishing Co., 1979.

Published posthumously in 1861, these studies of Matthew 1–16 contain the same richness of thought and close attention to details which readers of Alexander's other works have come to expect from this great Princeton professor.   226.2'07.AL2 1979

*Barber, Cyril John. *Vital Encounter: First-Century Encounters with Jesus Christ and Their Relevance for Us Today.* San Bernardino, CA: Here's Life Publishers, 1979.

Practical application of biblical truth derived from the lives of those who came into contact with Christ during His earthly ministry. Designed for adult Bible discussion groups.
                              225.92.B23 1979

Brown, Raymond E. *The Community of the Beloved Disciple*. New York: Paulist Press, 1979.

†This story of Johannine ecclesiology attempts to reconstruct the church of the first century, and seeks to glean from the apostle's writings principles that may apply to the church today.   226.5'082.B81

Bruce, Frederick Fyvie. *Peter, Stephen, James, and John: Studies in Early Non-Pauline Christianity*. Grand Rapids: Wm. B. Eerdmans Publishing Co., 1979.

Assesses the leadership of the men "at the helm" of affairs and their rejection of Judaism.
                              225.92.B83

Carson, David A. *The Farewell Discourse and Final Prayer of Jesus: An Exposition of John 14–17*. Grand Rapids: Baker Book House, 1980.

Brief, pertinent expository studies on a vital section of John's gospel. Readable and clear, combining exegesis with the timely application of the truth.   226.5'07.C23 14–17

*Gloag, Paton James. *A Critical and Exegetical Commentary on the Acts of the Apostles*. 2 vols. Minneapolis: Klock and Klock Christian Publishers, 1979.

H. B. Hackett wrote appreciatively of the work: "I have examined it with special care. For my purposes I have found it unsurpassed by any similar work in the English language. It shows a thoroughly mastery of the material, philology, history, and literature pertaining to this range of study, and a skill in the use of this knowledge, which places it in the first class of modern expositions." We concur.
                              226.6'07.G51 1979

*Godet, Frederic Louis. *Commentary on John's Gospel*. Grand Rapids: Kregel Publications, 1978.

One of the finest treatments of John's Gospel ever produced.   226.5'07.G54 1978

Hengel, Martin. *Acts and History of Earliest Christianity*. Translated by J. Bowden. Philadelphia: Fortress Press, 1980.

†Asserts the essential reliability of the Book of Acts and examines Luke's historical-theological methodology.   226.6'06.H38

*Hengstenberg, Ernst Wilhelm. *Commentary on the Gospel of St. John*. 2 vols. Minneapolis: Klock and Klock Christian Publishers, 1980.

Rich in grammatical and syntactical insights, this reverent and devout work ably treats the life and labors of the Lord Jesus Christ.   226.5'07.H38 1980.

Hultgren, Arland J. *Jesus and His Adversaries: The Form and Function of the Conflict Stories in the Synoptic Tradition*. Minneapolis: Augsburg Publishing House, 1979.

†This scholarly form-critical work draws attention to the confrontation of Christ with the Pharisees, Sadducees, etc. So much stress is placed on the literary form that the historic significance and importance of the events in Christ's life are obscured.   232.95.H87

MacArthur, John, Jr. *Kingdom Living Here and Now*. Chicago: Moody Press, 1980.

Representing expository preaching at its best, these sermons on the Beatitudes of Matthew 5 will challenge and edify the reader in much the same way they did when MacArthur's congregation first heard them.
                              226.9'07.M11

Morrison, George H. *Luke*. 2 vols. Chattanooga, TN: AMG Publishers, 1978.

Must rank among the finest expository sermons on Luke's Gospel ever published. As Alexander Maclaren in his *Exposition of Holy Scripture*, Morrison does not cover every verse.   226.4'07.M83

———. *Matthew*. 3 vols. Chattanooga, TN: AMG Publishers, 1978.

These eloquent messages expound the meaning of Matthew's Gospel with a force that is both compelling and persuasive.
                              226.2'06.M83

———. *Mark*. Ridgefield, NJ: AMG Publishers, 1978.

One of the giants of the Scottish pulpit,

Morrison's persuasive handling of Scripture attracted large crowds, and few who heard him remained unmoved. 226.3'07.M83

_____. *John*. Chattanooga, TN: AMG Publishers, 1978.
Preachers will find these brief expository studies to be masterpieces of the homiletic art. Valuable for their insights.
226.5'07.M83

*Pentecost, John Dwight. *The Sermon on the Mount: Contemporary Insights for a Christian Lifestyle*. Portland, OR: Multnomah Press, 1980.
First published under the title *Design for Living*, these expository messages adequately interpret Christ's words before applying His teaching to the lives of believers today. Recommended. 226.9'07.P38 1980

*Toussaint, Stanley Dale. *Behold the King: A Study of Matthew*. Portland, OR: Multnomah Press, 1980.

A work which expounds the theme of Matthew's Gospel with a thorough grounding in the exegesis of the text. Toussaint's exposition demonstrates that Jesus is indeed the Messiah, the King of Israel, and he describes the kingdom purpose in this portion of God's Word as no one else has yet done. Excellent.
226.02'7.T64

White, Reginald Ernest Oscar. *The Mind of Matthew*. Philadelphia: Westminster Press, 1979.
While using the form-critical approach to Matthew's Gospel, the author nevertheless has grasped the thematic structure of the evangelist's narrative and explains his theme accordingly. 226.2'06.W58

Wilcock, Michael. *The Savior of the World: The Message of Luke's Gospel*. Downers Grove, IL: InterVarsity Press, 1979.
A clear evangelical exposition of this Gospel. Avoids stereotypes and provides some helpful insights into Luke's special interests and style. 226.4'07.W64

Pauline Studies and the Pauline Epistles

*Bernard, John Henry. *The Pastoral Epistles*. Grand Rapids: Baker Book House, 1980.
First published in the Cambridge Greek Testament series in 1899, this exegetical study is preceded by a lengthy introduction. A critical edition of the Greek Scripture follows, and then a word-by-word or phrase-by-phrase exposition of the text. Excellent.
227.83'07.B45

Bruce, Frederick Fyvie. *1 and 2 Corinthians*. New Century Bible Commentary. Grand Rapids: Wm. B. Eerdmans Publishing Co., 1980.
First published in 1971, this brief, perceptive study aims at the elucidation of words or phrases and pays little or no attention to the theme of the epistle. 227.2'07.B83 1980

*Cranfield, Charles E. B. *A Critical and Exegetical Commentary on the Epistle to the Romans*, Vol. 2. International Critical Commentary. Edinburgh: T. and T. Clark, 1979.
Covers chapters 9–16. Includes an essay on Paul's purposes in writing Romans and some remarks on the theology of this Epistle. Must rank as one of the finest exegetical treatments available. 227.1'07.C85 v. 2

Demarest, Gary W. *Colossians: The Mystery of Christ in Us*. Waco, TX: Word Books, 1979.
Designed for discussion groups, this study is partly expository and partly sermonic. Does stress the centrality of Christ in Christian experience. 227.7'07.D39

*Edwards, Thomas Charles. *A Commentary on the First Epistle to the Corinthians*. Minneapolis: Klock and Klock Christian Publishers, 1980.
Combines solid exegesis with satisfying exposition to make a commentary that at once exemplifies the commentator's art. Adequately explains the apostle's theme. Deserving of an honored place in every pastor-teacher's library. 227.2'07.ED9 1980

*Fairbairn, Patrick. *The Pastoral Epistles*. Minneapolis: Klock and Klock Christian Publishers, 1980.
A particularly appropriate reprint in light of the fact that so many men are leaving the ministry on account of its unusual pressures. Provides a delightful example of exegesis aiding the exposition of the text.
227.83'07.F15 1980

*Gromacki, Robert Glenn. *Stand Fast in Liberty: An Exposition of Galatians*. Grand Rapids: Baker Book House, 1979.
Grounded in the historical setting of the people to whom Paul wrote, this study describes in a nontechnical way the meaning and message of this letter. Based upon the text of the KJV.   227.4'07.G89

*_____. *Stand Firm in the Faith: An Exposition of II Corinthians*. Grand Rapids: Baker Book House, 1979.
A well-balanced exposition using the text of the AV. Excellent treatment of Paul's theme. Gives evidence of Gromacki's exemplary use of the original text. Recommended.
227.3'07.G89

*_____. *Stand United in Joy: An Exposition of Philippians*. Grand Rapids: Baker Book House, 1980.
Adheres to the format established in the author's other NT commentaries. Ideal for personal or group Bible study. Nontechnical.
227.6'07.G89

*Hendriksen, William. *Exposition of Paul's Epistle to the Romans*, Vol. I. New Testament Commentary. Grand Rapids: Baker Book House, 1980.
A masterful commentary which will take its place among the leading expositions on this portion of the Pauline corpus. Recommended.   227.1'07.H38 v.1

*Hodge, Charles. *An Exposition of the First Epistle to the Corinthians*. Grand Rapids: Baker Book House, 1980.
Reprinted from the 1857 edition, this important exposition of the doctrine contained in this epistle explains the essence of church member effectiveness, enlarges on the nature of Christian liberty, and discusses the principles and practice of Christian assembly.
227.2'07.H66 1980

*_____. *An Exposition of the Second Epistle to the Corinthians*. Grand Rapids: Baker Book House, 1980.
First published in 1859, this doctrinal commentary demonstrates the importance of exegesis in proper biblical exposition. Also reveals the many facets of the apostle Paul's ministry.   227.3'07.H66 1980

Houlden, James Leslie. *Paul's Letters from Prison: Philippians, Colossians, Philemon, and Ephesians*. Westminster Pelican Commentaries. Philadelphia: Westminster Press, 1980.
†An exacting work which approaches matters of authorship, date, etc., critically. High-

lights the different purpose of each letter. Of value for its exegetical insights. Must be read with discernment.   227.6'07.H81

Howard, George. *Paul: Crisis in Galatia; A Study in Early Christian Theology*. Cambridge: Cambridge University Press, 1979.
Intertwines Paul's teaching of justification by faith with the universal blessings of the Abrahamic Covenant. Identifies Paul's opponents in Galatia as Jewish Christians from Jerusalem, and offers some well-researched ideas regarding Paul's view of the Mosaic law and the liberty believers enjoy in Christ.
227.4'06.H83

Jewett, Robert. *A Chronology of Paul's Life*. Philadelphia: Fortress Press, 1979.
†A scholarly assessment of the sources of chronology together with the fixed and discernible dates of Paul's life and ministry. Offers some new ideas and pinpoints with great detail the apostle's travel schedules and missionary activities.   225.9'24.J55

Käsemann, Ernst. *Commentary on Romans*. Translated and ed. by G. W. Bromiley. Grand Rapids: Wm. B. Eerdmans Publishing Co., 1980.
Clearly outlined and well documented, this scholarly commentary expands our awareness of Pauline theology. Reflects an individualism which necessitates reading with discernment.   227.1'07.K11

Keck, Leander E. *Paul and His Letters*. Philadelphia: Fortress Press, 1979.
Treats the major issues in Pauline studies, his message apart from the controversies which marked his ministry, and the fundamental issues which he taught and defended.
227'.06.K24

Knight, George W., III. *The Faithful Sayings in the Pastoral Letters*. Grand Rapids: Baker Book House, 1979.
This monograph expounds the repetitious statements "faithful is the saying . . ." and "worthy of all acceptation" in the Pastoral Epistles. Knight concludes that these statements form the self-conscious creedal/liturgical expression of the early church.
227'.06.K74

*Lightfoot, Joseph Barber. *Notes on the Epistles of St. Paul*. Winona Lake, IN: Alpha Publications, 1979.
Covers I and II Thessalonians, I Corinthians 1–7, Romans 1–7, and Ephesians 1. Follows the format of Lightfoot's other monumental works. Similar in format to the expository

and exegetical notes of F. J. A. Hort.
227'.07.L62 1979

*Lloyd-Jones, David Martyn. *The Unsearchable Riches of Christ: An Exposition of Ephesians 3:1-21*. Grand Rapids: Baker Book House, 1980.
Probing deeply into Paul's thought, Lloyd-Jones expounds the essence of the apostle's teaching and explains how Christians may know the true God as opposed to worshiping and serving a god of their own making.
227.5'07.L77 3 1980

Lucas, R. C. *Fullness and Freedom: The Message of Colossians and Philemon*. The Bible Speaks Today. Downers Grove, IL: InterVarsity Press, 1980.
Omits introductory matters and launches straight into an exposition of the text. Designed for expository preachers, but has value for personal study. 227.7'07.L96

McDonald, Hugh Dermot. *Commentary on Colossians and Philemon*. Waco, TX: Word Books, 1980.
A verse-by-verse treatment which, while nontechnical, will satisfy the needs of the seminarian and delight the lay Bible student.
227.7'07.M14

*Milligan, George. *St. Paul's Epistles to the Thessalonians*. Minneapolis: Klock and Klock Christian Publishers, 1980.
A rare work, ably combining scholarship with an explanation of the apostle's theme and purpose. Amillennial.
227.81'07.M62 1980

Robinson, John Arthur Thomas. *Wrestling with Romans*. Philadelphia: Westminster Press, 1979.
†A popular presentation which aims at making the apostle Paul's purpose understandable to intelligent laypeople. Uneven in

treatment and unreliable in theology.
227.1'07.R56

Sandmel, Samuel. *The Genius of Paul*. Philadelphia: Fortress Press, 1979.
First published in 1958, this informative study of a Jew by a Jew reveals an appreciation of the apostle without giving evidence of sharing his faith in Jesus as the Messiah. Seeks to correct errors the author has discerned in Davies' book *Paul and Rabbinic Judaism*. 227.092.P28.S5

Stanley, Arthur Peurhyn. *The Epistles of St. Paul to the Corinthians*. 2d ed. Minneapolis: Klock and Klock Christian Publishers, 1981.
A scholarly, critical study of the setting and text of these letters. Follows the format of Lightfoot's studies, with "dissertations" on different ideas requiring greater extrapolation. 227.2'07.ST2 1981

*Stott, John Robert Walmsey. *God's New Society: The Message of Ephesians*. The Bible Speaks Today. Downers Grove, IL: InterVarsity Press, 1979.
A delightful exposition. At once timely and relevant; an example of expository preaching at its best. Buy it and read it . . . often.
227.5'07.S7

Taylor, Thomas. *Exposition of Titus*. Minneapolis: Klock and Klock Christian Publishers, 1980.
A Puritan commentary which readily explores the inner reality of Paul's letter to his youthful associate. 227.85'07.T21 1980

*Westcott, Brooke Foss. *Saint Paul's Epistle to the Ephesians*. Grand Rapids: Baker Book House, 1979.
In spite of its age, this exegetical study deserves repeated consultation by all who wish to become familiar with the apostle Paul's thought and theology. 227.5'07.W52 1979

General Epistles

Boice, James Montgomery. *The Epistles of John*. Grand Rapids: Zondervan Publishing House, 1979.
Boice finds the theme of I John to be "Christian Assurance" rather than fellowship, and he expounds John's writings accordingly. II and III John are seen as repeating the general message of the first

epistle. In general, a valuable contribution.
227.94'07.B63

Brown, John. *Parting Counsels: An Exposition of 2 Peter 1*. Edinburgh: Banner of Truth Trust, 1980.
First published in 1856, this study was cut short due to the author's death. The material

covering chapter 1 (more than 300 pages) is rich, clear, and worthy of attention.

227.93'07.B81 1 1980

Bruce, Alexander Balmain. *The Epistle to the Hebrews: The First Apology for Christianity; an Exegetical Study.* Minneapolis: Klock and Klock Christian Publishers, 1980.
In 21 chapters, Bruce treats the theology and message of this epistle. All things considered, this work is a masterful combination of sound exegesis and exposition. Reformed.

227.87'07.B83 1980

Bullinger, Ethelbert William. *Great Cloud of Witnesses in Hebrews Eleven.* Grand Rapids: Kregel Publishers, 1979.
A careful exegetical study which succeeds in examining the life and labors, trials and triumphs of those "heroes of the faith" whose witness is forever inscribed in Hebrews 11.

227.87'06.B87 11 1979.

Candlish, Robert Smith. *First Epistle of John.* Grand Rapids: Kregel Publications, 1979.
A true classic. Rich in insights; rewarding reading. Reprinted from the 1877 edition.

227.94'07.C16 1979.

Goudge, William. *Commentary on Hebrews, Exegetical and Expository.* Grand Rapids: Kregel Publications, 1980.
A monumental work by a Puritan divine who ministered at Blackfriar's in London for 45 years. A member of the Westminster Assembly of Divines, Goudge expounded the Epistle to the Hebrews over a 30-year period at weekly Bible readings. Spurgeon esteemed this work "a great prize."

227.87'07.G72 1980

Hughes, Graham. *Hebrews and Hermeneutics: The Epistle to the Hebrews as a New Testament Example of Biblical Interpretation.* Cambridge: Cambridge University Press, 1979.

In this important contribution to the difficult subject of biblical interpretation, Hughes builds upon the thesis that the author of Hebrews was trying to establish a theological understanding of the relationship between the outmoded forms and institutions of OT ritual and worship and the distinctions of the person and work of Christ. Interesting, but misleading.   227.87'063.H87

Laws, Sophie. *A Commentary on the Epistle of James.* Harper's New Testament Commentaries. San Francisco: Harper and Row, 1980.
†Grounds her understanding of the Epistle of James in the attitude of Jewish Christians of the times. Sees James taking issue with the apostle Paul and Pauline tradition.

227.91'07.L44

Plummer, Alfred. *The Epistles of St. John.* Grand Rapids: Baker Book House, 1980.
This reprint of the 1886 commentary from the Cambridge Greek Testament readily interacts with the critical issues raised by the texts of Tischendorf and Tregelles, and then treats the data of these letters in a most commendable way. Recommended.

227.94'07.P73 1980

Stedman, Ray C. *Expository Studies in I John: Life By the Son.* Waco, TX: Word Books, 1980.
An outstanding exposition which explains the heart of John's message and applies it with verve to the life of believers and the church today. Recommended.   227.94'07.S3

Stier, Rudolf. *Commentary On James.* Lynchburg, VA: James Family Publishers, 1979.
Long out of print, and formerly published with *The Words of the Apostles* (1864), these fine expository messages adequately treat this important epistle.   227.91'07.S5

Revelation

Coleman, Robert Emerson. *Songs of Heaven.* Old Tappan, NJ: Fleming H. Revell Company, 1980.
A unique devotional study of the "songs heard around the throne" in John's vision of heaven contained in the Book of Revelation. Provides a pattern of worship for God's peo-

ple here on earth as well as in the hereafter.

228'.06.C67

Court, John M. *Myth and History in the Book of Revelation.* Atlanta: John Knox Press, 1979.
A brief literary and historical approach to

John's apocalypse which focuses on seven key themes as the basis for a new understanding of this portion of Scripture. 228'.06.C83

Sweet, John Philip McMurdo. *Revelation*. Westminster Pelican Commentaries. Phila-delphia: Westminster Press, 1979.

Views the contents of John's vision as a series of historically unrelated events—past, present, and future intertwined. Of value for the writer's information on Hebrew imagery. 228'.07.S3 1979

Chapter 5

DOCTRINAL THEOLOGY

Systems of Theology

Barth, Karl. *The Doctrine of the Word of God.* Vol. 1, Pt. 1: Church Dogmatics. Translated by G. W. Bromiley. Edinburgh: T. and T. Clark, 1975.

A fresh translation demonstrating that, in the forty years since the first English edition, Barth's fame has not waned and his value as a theologian has increased. Neo-orthodox.
230'.41.B28

Battles, Ford Lewis, and **John Walchenbach.** *Analysis of the Institutes of the Christian Religion of John Calvin.* Grand Rapids: Baker Book House, 1980.

Based on lectures delivered at the Pittsburgh Theological Seminary, this analysis serves to introduce students to the 1559 edition of the *Institutes*. A worthy acquisition.
230'.42.C13.B31

Berkhof, Hendrikus. *Christian Faith: An Introduction to the Study of the Faith.* Translated by S. Woudstra. Grand Rapids: Wm. B. Eerdmans Publishing Co., 1979.

Not a theology in the traditional sense, but rather a series of brief, scholarly essays on a variety of theological themes covering revelation to eschatology and including excursuses into the nature of the people of Israel and the "new community." Reformed.
230'.232.B45 1979

Bromiley, Geoffrey William. *An Introduction to the Theology of Karl Barth.* Grand Rapids: Wm. B. Eerdmans Publishing Co., 1979.

An introduction to Barth's *Kirchliche Dogmatik.* Balanced and judicious.
230'.41.B28.B78

Gratsch, Edward J., ed. *Principles of Catholic Theology.* Staten Island, NY: Alba House, 1981.

One of the best syntheses of Catholic theology in the post-Vatican II era. Well documented.
230'.2.G77

Greaves, Richard L. *Theology and Resolution in the Scottish Reformation: Studies in the Thought of John Knox.* Grand Rapids: Wm. B. Eerdmans Publishing Co., 1980.

Draws attention to John Knox's theology but, while elaborating upon the major themes undergirding his beliefs, fails to treat all aspects of the Scot's thought.
230'.52.K77.G79

Klotsche, E. H. *The History of Christian Doctrine.* Revised ed. Grand Rapids: Baker Book House, 1979.

First published in 1945, this able Lutheran work traces the development of doctrine from the apostolic age to the present. Well outlined.
230'.09.K69 1979

Niesel, Wilhelm. *The Theology of Calvin.* Translated by H. Knight. Grand Rapids: Baker Book House, 1980.

First published in German in 1938, this detailed study of Calvin's system of theology deals concisely with the knowledge of God, the Trinity, creation and providence, sin, the law of God, etc. 230'.42.C13.N55

Thiessen, Henry Clarence. *Lectures in Systematic Theology.* Revised by Vernon D. Doerksen. Grand Rapids: Wm. B. Eerdmans Publishing Co., 1979.

First published thirty years ago, this exemplary introductory study of theology retains the same format as the original work with the exception of a new chapter on the work of the Holy Spirit. Many sections have been reworded and outdated material has been eliminated. 230'.5.T34D 1979

Special Topics

Bonhoeffer, Dietrich. *Christ the Center.* Translated by E. H. Robertson. San Francisco: Harper and Row, 1978.
Constructed from lecture notes by Eberhard Bethge and published in English in 1966. Stimulating, Christocentric, Neo-orthodox.
230.8.B64 1978.

Cherry, Conrad. *Nature and Religious Imagination: From Edwards to Bushnell.* Philadelphia: Fortress Press, 1980.
Absorption with nature during the eighteenth and early nineteenth centuries captured the interest of scholars in all areas of academic pursuit. This work surveys the contribution of theologians to this subject during that period.
230'.08.C42

Coleman, Richard J. *Issues of Theological Conflict, Revised: Evangelicals and Liberals.* Grand Rapids: Wm. B. Eerdmans Publishing Co., 1980.
Previously published as *Issues of Theological Warfare* (1972), this work in its revised format continues to provide a forum for discussion between liberals and evangelicals. Its weaknesses, however, while less apparent, are still in evidence. Ignores the Bible's own testimony to the supernatural. The goal of "forging middle ground" can only be accomplished through compromise on the part of those who are thorough evangelicals.
230'.08.C67 1980

Custance, Arthur C. *The Sovereignty of Grace.* Grand Rapids: Baker Book House, 1979.
A full, historically complete discussion of the "five points of Calvinism" with a concluding section in which Custance inveighs against those who only partially adhere to these tenets of Reformed doctrine.
230'.08.C83.C96

Duncan, Homer. *Secular Humanism: The Most Dangerous Religion in America.* Lubbock, TX: Missionary Crusader, 1980.
"This fact-filled book should alert intelligent Americans concerning the cancer of Secular Humanism. It deals with the cause rather than the symptoms of moral decline."
144.D91

Fuller, Daniel P. *Gospel and Law: Contrast or Continuum? The Hermeneutics of Dispensationalism and Covenant Theology.* Grand

Rapids: Wm. B. Eerdmans Publishing Co., 1980.
A disappointing, biased treatment which misrepresents the issues. Lacks a solid biblical foundation and confuses the issues of law and grace.
230.8.C83.F95

Geisler, Norman Leo, and **Paul David Feinberg.** *Introduction to Philosophy: A Christian Perspective.* Grand Rapids: Baker Book House, 1980.
A fine text which ably sifts through the maze of human theories and systems, and provides a clear, concise, and convincing approach to philosophy.
101.G27

***Hanna, Mark M.** *Crucial Questions in Apologetics.* Grand Rapids: Baker Book House, 1981.
Seeks to resolve the deadlock between presuppositionism and verificationism by developing an epistemological approach to the search for truth which preserves the distinctiveness of special revelation.
239.H19

Henry, Carl Ferdin and Howard. *The God Who Speaks and Shows:* Vols. 3 and 4, *God, Revelation and Authority.* Waco, TX: Word Books, 1979.
These volumes are part of Henry's *magnum opus.* In them he lays down fifteen theses about inspiration, revelation, and biblical authority. Stating emphatically that revelation culminates in Christ, Henry uses Christology as the basis of his apologetic.
230'.08.H39

Kantzer, Kenneth S., and **Stanley N. Gundry,** eds. *Perspectives on Evangelical Theology.* Grand Rapids: Baker Book House, 1979.
Comprising papers read at the Thirtieth Annual Meeting of the Evangelical Theological Society, these studies treat facets of systematic, biblical, philosophical, and pastoral theology.
230'.08.EV1 1979

***McDowell, Josh,** comp. *Evidence That Demands a Verdict: Historical Evidences for the Christian Faith.* Revised ed. San Bernardino, CA: Here's Life Publishers, 1979.
A handy work covering bibliology, Christology, eschatology, and human experience. Provides ready access to a variety of source materials.
239.M14 1979.

Oden, Thomas C. *Agenda for Theology.* San Francisco: Harper and Row, 1979.

†Discusses the dilemmas facing quasi-orthodox theologians and challenges them with the need for pastoral and sociological relevance. Makes stimulating reading.
230'.08.OD2

Sponheim, Paul R. *Faith and Process: The Significance of Process Thought for Christian Faith.* Minneapolis: Augsburg Publishing House, 1979.
Grounds his thesis in the philosophical views of Alfred North Whitehead and, by availing himself of the contribution of theologians such as Hartshorne, Cobb, Ogden, and others, attempts to integrate metaphysics and Christian belief.
230.08.S6

Stater, Peter. *The Dynamics of Religion: Meaning and Change in Religious Traditions.* San Francisco: Harper and Row, 1978.
Much of the book is devoted to questions of meaning regarding symbols, stories, and patterns of change in different religions.
201.S2

Toon, Peter. *Free to Obey: The Real Meaning of Authority.* Wheaton, IL: Tyndale House Publishers, 1979.
Treats clearly and concisely the fact of sin and the enslavement of mankind to it. Explains the only path to perfect freedom. Recommended.
220.1.T61

Webber, Robert E. *God Still Speaks: A Biblical View of Christian Communication.* Nashville: Thomas Nelson Publishers, 1980.
This theological discussion of communication places emphasis on the church, its people, and mission. Techniques of communication are an integral part of Webber's discussion and are based solidly on the teaching of Scripture. Recommended.
230'.01.W38

Godhead

God, Attributes

*Charnock, Stephen.** *Discourses upon the Existence and Attributes of God.* 2 vols. Grand Rapids: Baker Book House, 1979.
Reprinted from an 1853 edition, these sermons comprise one of the ablest and fullest expositions of this aspect of theology. Highly recommended.
231.4.C38 1979

*Hook, H. Philip.** *Who Art in Heaven.* Grand Rapids: Zondervan Publishing House, 1979.
With devotion and skill the author discusses the attributes of God and then applies the truths gleaned from Scripture to the relationship of the believer with the members of the Godhead. Ideal for adult discussion groups.
231.4.H76

*Houston, James M.** *I Believe in the Creator.* Grand Rapids: Wm. B. Eerdmans Publishing Co., 1980.
While all evangelicals will not agree with everything Houston writes, he has made a fine contribution to an understanding of the doctrine of creation, Christ's role as originator and sustainer of the universe, and the relationship of His creatures to Himself.
231.7.H81

Toon, Peter. *God Here and Now: The Christian View of God.* Wheaton, IL: Tyndale House Publishers, 1979.
Builds upon an understanding of God's attributes and describes the process whereby the Christian, having been brought by God into a relationship with Himself, may now enjoy continuing fellowship with Him. Recommended.
231.T61

Jesus Christ

Barnes, Albert. *The Atonement.* Minneapolis: Bethany Fellowship, 1980.
Published in 1860, this logically reasoned, biblically based discussion of the atonement answers objections and demonstrates clearly the imperative necessity of Christ's death. Lacks Scripture, subject, and author indices. Presbyterian.
232.2.B26

Bruce, Frederick Fyvie. *What the Bible Teaches About What Jesus Did.* Wheaton, IL: Tyndale House Publishers, 1979.
Designed for lay people, this slender volume covers the important events in Christ's life and ministry, and discusses their relevance to the believer.
232.95.B83

Buell, Jon A., and **O. Quentin Hyder.** *Jesus: God, Ghost or Guru?* Grand Rapids: Zondervan Publishing House, 1978.
A careful inquiry into Jesus' claims to be the Messiah. Well reasoned. Of apologetic value.   232.954.B86

Goulder, Michael, ed. *Incarnation and Myth.* Grand Rapids: Wm. B. Eerdmans Publishing Co., 1979.
Furthers the discussion begun in *The Myth of God Incarnate* (1977). Evangelical contributors are conspicuous by their absence.
232.1.IN2 1979.

Habermas, Gary R. *The Resurrection of Jesus.* Grand Rapids: Baker Book House, 1980.
This serious discussion of the theology of the resurrection relates the reality of Christ's *anastasis* to one's view of the world in which we live, the inspiration of Scripture, and eternal life. A concluding chapter is concerned with the Holy Spirit and the development of a biblical system of apologetics.   232.5.H11

Hunter, Archibald Macbride. *Christ and the Kingdom.* Ann Arbor, MI: Servant Books, 1980.
Probes the essence of the theocracy in the teaching of Jesus and points out that those belonging to the kingdom should be characterized by a radically different lifestyle.
232.954.H91

*Liddon, Henry Parry**, and **James Orr.** *The Birth of Christ.* Minneapolis: Klock and Klock Christian Publishers, 1980.
Combines Liddon's exposition of Luke 1 with Orr's fine study of the virgin conception of Christ. These works ably complement each other.   232.921.L61 1980

Milligan, William. *The Ascension of Christ.* Minneapolis: Klock and Klock Christian Publishers, 1980.
Combines excellence in presentation with accuracy in interpretation to make this study of Christ's post-resurrection and present heavenly ministries a book which all Christians will enjoy reading.   232.973.M62 1980.

*Moule, Handley Carr Glyn**, and **James Orr.** *The Resurrection of Christ.* Minneapolis: Klock and Klock Christian Publishers, 1980.
Combines Moule's inimitable exposition of John 20-21 with Orr's theological treatise. Together these works provide pastors and students with a rare combination of excellence in exposition coupled with a clear enunciation of theological truth. 232.97.M86 1980

Smeaton, George. *The Doctrine of the Atonement as Taught by Christ Himself.* Winona Lake, IN: Alpha Publications, 1979.
First published in 1871, this exegetical work by a British Reformed scholar contains a substantive treatment of Christ's own teaching on His death, the application of the benefits of His atonement to "the Church," and the effects of the atonement on the saved and unsaved.   232.3.S3C 1979.

Tenney, Merrill Chapin. *Who's Boss?* Wheaton, IL: Victor Books, 1980.
Zeroes in on the questions Christ asked during His ministry and shows how they deal with the issues of life which still are of concern to people today.   232'.09.T25

Toon, Peter. *Jesus Christ is Lord.* Valley Forge, PA: Judson Press, 1979.
A popular presentation of the exaltation of Jesus Christ as Lord. Episcopalian. 232.T61

Holy Spirit

Bullinger, Ethelbert William. *The Giver and His Gifts, or the Holy Spirit and His Work.* Grand Rapids: Kregel Publications, 1979.
Building his theology upon a careful investigation of the Hebrew and Greek words for "spirit," Bullinger provides a penetrating study of the biblical teaching. Ultradispensational.   231.3.B87 1979

Moule, Charles Francis Digby. *The Holy Spirit.* Grand Rapids: Wm. B. Eerdmans Publishing Co., 1979.
Complete with the wisdom and spiritual insight which we have come to expect of the author, we find in these seven chapters a contemporary discussion of the relationship of the Holy Spirit to specific areas of theology and ministry. A final chapter deals with the charismatic question.   231.3.M86

Schweizer, Edward. *The Holy Spirit.* Translated by R. H. and I. Fuller. Philadelphia: Fortress Press, 1980.
†Avoids treating the Paraclete as a person. Investigates the roles of the Spirit in both Testaments and in the intertestamental period.
231'.3.SCH9

White, Reginald Ernest Oscar. *The Answer Is the Spirit.* Philadelphia: Westminster Press, 1979.
In keeping with the form-critical approach used in the writer's other books, this treatment of the teaching on the ministry of the Holy Spirit gives evidence of the extent to which this British Baptist has been influenced by biblical criticism.   231.3.W58

Man

Brand, Paul, and **Philip Yancey.** *Fearfully and Wonderfully Made*. Grand Rapids: Zondervan Publishing House, 1980.

Discusses the marvels of God's handiwork in the human body. C. Everett Koop said this work is "A unique book . . . that alternates from dazzling descriptions of the function of various parts of the human body in layman's terms to analyses of the form and function of the Body of Christ . . . an enthralling edifying book which I wish I had had the insight to write."   233.B73

Hardy, Alister. *The Spiritual Nature of Man: A Study of Contemporary Religious Experience*. Oxford: Clarendon Press, 1979.

An historic record of the work by the Religious Experience Research Unit, Oxford. Darwinian in approach; believes man's spiritual nature is intimately linked with the "evolutionary" process.   291.4'2.H22

MacKay, Donald M. *Human Science and Human Dignity*. Downers Grove, IL: InterVarsity Press, 1979.

Grounded solidly in the Scriptures, this plea for an authentic humanness penetrates through the "froth and bubble" of behaviorism and humanism and genetic manipulation. Develops a unique interdisciplinary view of the *imago Dei*.   233.M19

Packer, James Innell. *Knowing Man*. Westchester, IL: Cornerstone Books, 1979.

In a series of direct, pointed messages, Packer treats the true humanity of man in his relation to God, society, and others. Clarifies much of the confusion interjected into the discussion of anthropology by those who do not adhere to biblical revelation.   233.P12

Salvation

Anderson, Robert. *Redemption Truths*. Grand Rapids: Kregel Publications, 1980.

Published soon after the turn of the century under the title *For Us Men*, these chapters unfold the doctrine of salvation showing, as best man can, the marvels of God's plan for our redemption. Well done; stimulating.
                     234.AN2R 1980

*****Boice, James Montgomery.** *Awakening to God*. Vol. III, Foundations of the Christian Life. Downers Grove, IL: InterVarsity Press, 1979.

Continues the series of doctrinal issues for laypeople. Discusses the work of the Holy Spirit in the salvation of the repentant sinner and provides an excellent treatment of key issues of justification, adoption, sanctification, etc. Recommended.   234.B63

Bray, Gerald Lewis. *Holiness and the Will of God: Perspectives on the Theology of Tertullian*. Atlanta: John Knox Press, 1979.

Emphasizing the theme of holiness, this survey of Tertullian's teaching on the subject serves to bring into perspective the historic setting which gave rise to his views. An excellent treatment.   234.8'09.T27.B73

Burkhardt, Helmut. *The Biblical Doctrine of Regeneration*. Translated by O. R. John-

ston. Downers Grove, IL: InterVarsity Press, 1978.

Builds upon the meaning of the biblical terminology and notes that this doctrine is seldom considered by contemporary theologians. Traces the history of the concept of regeneration and its importance in the teaching of evangelical churches.   234.4.B91

Erickson, Millard J., ed. *The New Life: Readings in Christian Theology*. Grand Rapids: Baker Book House, 1979.

This anthology is designed to serve as a companion volume to *The Living God* and *Man's Need and God's Gift*. Contains essays by a wide variety of post-Reformation scholars.   234.ER4

Gillespie, Virgil Bailey. *Religious Conversion and Personal Identity: How and Why People Change*. Birmingham, AL: Religious Education Press, 1979.

While not holding to an evangelical view of conversion, Gillespie treats the social, familial, theological, philosophical, or psychological reasons for religious change.   234.G41

Green, Edward Michael Bankes. *Faith For the Nonreligious*. Wheaton, IL: Tyndale House Publishers, 1979.

Deals with the typical excuses of the unsaved. Will give practical sidelights into how those in the church may deal with those whom they meet.   234.2.G82

Vander Lugt, Herbert. *God's Plan in All*

the Ages. Grand Rapids: Zondervan Publishing House, 1979.

Blends God's soteriological purpose for mankind with His theocracy. Informative. Designed for laypeople. Of value for adult study groups.   234.V28

Demonology

Alexander, William Menzies. *Demonic Possession in the New Testament: Its Historical, Medical, and Theological Aspects.* Grand Rapids: Baker Book House, 1980.

First published in 1902, this work, by a man holding doctorates in medicine, science, and theology, is valuable for its realistic appraisal of the teaching of the NT, and particularly as it relates to the increasing prevalence of the "powers of darkness" today.
235.4.AL2 1980

*Pink, Arthur Walkington.** *The Antichrist.* Minneapolis: Klock and Klock Christian

Publishers, 1979.

First published in 1923, these chapters provide one of the finest and most comprehensive overviews of the origin and identity character and destination of the "Man of Sin."
235.48.P65 1979.

Wiersbe, Warren W. *The Strategy of Satan: How to Detect and Defeat Him.* Wheaton, IL: Tyndale House Publishers, 1979.

Insightful chapters on Satan's personality, strategies, plans, and future destiny.
235.47.W63

Eschatology

Anderson, Robert. *Forgotten Truths.* Grand Rapids: Kregel Publications, 1980.

First published in 1914, this study directs the attention of readers to Israel, God's chosen people, and describes their role in the prophetic scriptures. Insightful.
236.3.AN2 1980

Bailey, Lloyd R. *Biblical Perspectives on Death.* Philadelphia: Fortress Press, 1979.

Surveys the variety of views on mortality found in the literature of the ancient Near East, the OT, intertestamental period, and the NT. Evaluates the biblical perspectives and applies the results to present-day circumstances.   237.1.B15

*Boice, James Montgomery.** *God and History.* Vol. IV, Foundations of the Christian Faith. Downers Grove, IL: InterVarsity Press, 1981.

Blends an awareness of time with future eschatological events and shows how the church, through its ministry, is able to meet the needs of the present while preparing for the future.   236.B63

Feinburg, Charles Lee. *Millennialism: The Two Major Views.* 3d enlarged ed. Chicago: Moody Press, 1980.

Contrasts the premillennial and amillennial systems of interpretation and critiques their eschatological strengths and weaknesses.
236.6.F32 1980.

Govett, Robert. *Entrance into the Kingdom, or Reward According to Works.* Miami Springs, FL: Conley and Schoettle Publishing Co., 1978.

Reprinted from the 1853 edition, this theological treatise discusses the position of the elect of God, the privileges of service, and the reward of their inheritance in Christ.

Gray, John. *The Biblical Doctrine of the Reign of God.* Edinburgh: T. and T. Clark, 1979.

†A detailed, scholarly discussion of the enthronement psalms and the messianic teaching of the post-exilic prophets. Traces the idea of the theocracy through the intertestamental period and the ministry of Jesus, and concludes with "The Reign of God in the Church." For the discerning reader.
236.1.G79

Jewett, Robert. *Jesus Against the Rapture: Seven Unexpected Prophecies.* Philadelphia: Westminster Press, 1979.

A vigorous rebuttal of premillennialism,

with a denunciation of Carl McIntyre, Hal Lindsay, Kenneth Kantzer, and others who look for Christ's return and the inauguration of His millennial reign. Jewett bases his views on seven NT passages.   236.3.J55

Kelsey, Morton T. *Afterlife: The Other Side of Dying.* New York: Paulist Press, 1979.
†This very full, extensively researched, moderately psychoanalytic, antisupernaturalistic treatise has been written in the wake of the plethora of "out-of-the-body" experiences recorded by those who "died," only to be resuscitated. The author attempts to walk a theological tightrope between modern parapsychology and the Scriptures. His material is presented well, but lacks conviction, particularly when dealing with heaven and hell.   237.2.K29

Peters, George Nathaniel Henry. *The Theocratic Kingdom of Our Lord Jesus the Christ, as Covenanted in the Old Testament and Presented in the New Testament.* Grand Rapids: Kregel Publications, 1979.
Originally published in 1884, this work ranks as one of the greatest studies on the interpretation of the prophetic word ever produced. Appears to favor a partial, midtribulation rapture. However, discourses at length on the theocratic kingdom concept contained in the Scriptures. Recommended.
236.P44 1979

Robinson, John Arthur Thomas. *Jesus and His Coming.* Philadelphia: Westminster Press, 1979.
Published in England in 1957, this treatment of *parousia* in the NT has a great deal to offer. Unfortunately, it has been written from a highly critical perspective and interprets the eschatological expectations of Christ and Paul in light of an assumed evolution of the theology of the early church. Disappointing.   232.6.R56 1979

Shedd, William Greenough Thayer. *The Doctrine of Endless Punishment.* Minneapolis: Klock and Klock Christian Publishers, 1980.
A well-reasoned, theologically accurate statement of the doctrine which treats fully,

yet concisely, the data contained in the Scriptures.   237.4.SH3 1980

Strauss, Lehman. *Prophetic Mysteries Revealed.* Neptune, NJ: Loizeaux Brothers, 1980.
Contains studies on Matthew 13 and Revelation 2–3. Premillenial. The excellence of these expository studies, in part, is minimized by the omission of a similar study covering Matthew 24–25 and Romans 9–11. Stimulating.   236.S8

Travis, Stephen H. *Christian Hope and the Future.* Downers Grove, IL: InterVarsity Press, 1980.
Directs the attention of readers to the leading issues of the last two decades. Probes the *parousia*, the resurrection of the dead, immortality, etc., and discusses the contributions of modern thinkers to eschatology.   236.T69

Vos, Geerhardus. *The Pauline Eschatology.* Grand Rapids: Baker Book House, 1979.
First published in 1930, this sequel to *The Kingdom and the Church* (1903) continues the author's treatment of redemptive history as found in Scripture and seeks to elucidate Paul's eschatology. Amillennial.
227.082.V92 1979

Walvoord, John Flipse. *The Rapture Question.* Revised and enlarged ed. Grand Rapids: Zondervan Publishing House, 1979.
A clear, definitive presentation of the biblical data pointing to a pretribulation rapture. This revised edition answers, briefly and concisely, some of the issues raised by Gundry in *The Church and the Tribulation.*
236.4.W17R 1979

Weber, Timothy P. *Living in the Shadow of the Second Coming: American Premillennialism, 1879-1925.* New York: Oxford University Press, 1979.
Based upon the author's doctoral dissertation, University of Chicago Divinity School, this scholarly, though biased, study purports to find the origins of premillennial thought in the Civil War and identifies adherents to the movement with a socio-economic group rather than the Scriptures.   236.3.AM3.W38

Chapter 6

DEVOTIONAL LITERATURE

Christian Ethics

Beauchamp, T. L., and **Norman E. Bowie**, eds. *Ethical Theory and Business*. Englewood Cliffs, NJ: Prentice-Hall, 1979.

Reviews representative viewpoints on currently controversial topics in business ethics and takes a fresh look at certain long-forgotten themes. 174.4.ET3

Catherwood, Henry Frederick Ross. *First Things First: The Ten Commandments in the 20th Century*. Downers Grove, IL: InterVarsity Press, 1979.

These studies, by a British politician, demonstrate not only the abiding relevance of the Decalogue, but also illustrate the necessity of men and nations living in accordance with its ethical teachings. 241.52.C28

Evans, Donald. *Struggle and Fulfillment: The Inner Dynamics of Religion and Morality*. Philadelphia: Fortress Press, 1979.

Designed to bridge the gap between religious belief and moral practice, this book discusses eight traits which, when transformed into virtues, have the ability to guide and govern one's conduct. 241.EV1

Forell, George Wolfgang. *History of Christian Ethics*. Vol. 1: *From the New Testament to Augustine*. Minneapolis: Augsburg Publishing House, 1979.

While commendable for its survey of the development of ethical theories, the reader is left with the impression that Forell's Neoorthodoxy has beclouded the issues and led to the development of a quasi-sophisticated theory in which the teaching of Scripture, even on the part of the early Church Fathers, is now distorted to fit a preconceived point of view. 241'.09.F76

Lande, Nathaniel, and **Afton Slade.** *Stages: Understanding How You Make Your Moral Decisions*. San Francisco: Harper and Row, 1979.

Describes the process by which ethical decisions are made and how a person may know right from wrong. Secular. 170.1'9.L23

Pinson, W. M., Jr., comp. *An Approach to Christian Ethics: The Life, Contribution and Thought of T. B. Matson*. Nashville: Broadman Press, 1979.

Essays by 23 Southern Baptists who comment on the influence of Thomas Buford Matson to themselves, others, churches, and the denomination. 241.B22A

Rudnick, Milton L. *Christian Ethics for Today: An Evangelical Approach*. Grand Rapids: Baker Book House, 1979.

Logical, but not necessarily biblical, this book traces the origin of the breakdown in ethical standards, the need for absolutes, and how the Christian community might regain the ground lost over the past four decades. Insightful. 241.R83

Shannon, Thomas A., and **James J. DiGiacomo.** *An Introduction to Bioethics*. New York: Paulist Press, 1979.

Contains pointed chapters on hotly debated topics: technology, abortion, genetic engineering, euthanasia, etc. Stimulating reading. 174.2.SH1

Simmons, Paul D., ed. *Issues in Christian Ethics*. Nashville: Broadman Press, 1980.

Essays by leading Southern Baptists. Well researched and informative. 241.S4 1980

Stendahl, Brita. *Sabbatical Reflections: The Ten Commandments in a New Day*. Philadelphia: Fortress Press, 1980.

A candid and refreshing discussion of the relevance of the Decalogue for life today. 248.4.S4

Stevens, Edwards. *Business Ethics*. New York: Paulist Press, 1979.

Traces the rise of modern ethical theory from Darwin's "Age of Survival," through Machiavelli's "Rule of Expediency," to the present. Informative, but lacking a solid biblical base. Roman Catholic.   174.4.S4

Thayer, Lee., comp. and ed. *Ethics, Morality, and the Media: Reflections on American Culture.* New York: Hastings House, 1980.

Answers the question about the impact of mass media on morals and values. Includes a consideration of economic and cultural issues as perceived by communication experts and sociologists. Explores the major moral issues and their impact on society of standards of journalism and public taste.
301.16.AM3.ET3

Christian Living

Augsburger, David, and **John Faul.** *Beyond Assertiveness.* Waco, TX: Word Books, 1980.
In the wake of books like *How to Win Through Intimidation*, two Christian psychologists show that there is more to being appropriately assertive than mastering a few techniques. Personal security is needed. This coverage of the issues is a decided step in the right direction.   158.1.AU4

Ausubel, David P. *What Every Well-Informed Person Should Know About Drug Addiction.* 2d ed. Chicago: Nelson-Hall, 1980.
First published in 1958, this work has justified its place in the bookmarket for its description of the problems that bring on drug addiction, the effects of drugs on users, and how drug users may be helped.
613.8'3.AU7 1980

Bloesch, Donald G. *The Struggle of Prayer.* San Francisco: Harper and Row, 1980.
A Neo-evangelical approach to prayer which, in spite of certain inherent weaknesses, seriously confronts the lack of prayer (lack of true spirituality) on the part of believers.   248.3'2.B62

Cavanagh, Michael E. *Make Your Tomorrow Better.* New York: Paulist Press, 1980.
Part of the growing corpus of books designed to assist people to understand themselves better by becoming more aware of their emotions. A most helpful treatise. 158.1.C31

Cedar, Paul A. *Seven Keys to Maximum Communication.* Wheaton, IL: Tyndale House Publishers, 1980.
Treats in simple terms the negative and positive feelings we all share—feelings which either erect walls between us or build bridges toward one another. Helpful.   001.5.C32

Chelune, Gordon J., et al. *Self-Disclosure: Origins, Patterns, and Implications of Openness in Interpersonal Relationships.* San Francisco: Jossey-Bass Publishers, 1979.

Pastors will be interested in this volume for its practical emphasis on personal growth and the dynamics of fellowship, much of which parallels the teaching of Scripture on the Body of Christ.   301.11.S4

Collins, Gary R. *The Joy of Caring.* Waco, TX: Word Books, 1980.
Collins treats the emotional responses common to all of us and points to the need for developing a caring community. He then shows how Christians may develop a genuine concern for others while avoiding the pitfalls of those who minister to others in order to meet a felt need of their own.   152.4.C69J

Cox-Gedmark, Jan. *Coping with Physical Disability.* Philadelphia: Westminster Press, 1980.
Continues the Christian Care Books series. Treats the problems and perplexities of the handicapped and shows how those in the church may reach out with love and acceptance. Should be in every church library.
248.8'6.C83

Crane, Thomas E. *Patterns of Biblical Spirituality.* Denville, NJ: Dimension Books, 1979.
This brief introduction to biblical spirituality begins with some general guidelines and then studies the experiences of men like Abraham, Moses, Jeremiah, the psalmists, Paul, and Mary. Stimulating reading. Roman Catholic.   248.4.C85

Dobson, James Clayton, Jr. *Emotions: Can You Trust Them?* Ventura, CA: Regal Books, 1980.
The excellence which we have come to associate with this writer's books is not in evidence here. Biblically, a case could have been made for two primary emotions: love and fear. A discussion of the negative relational emotions stemming from fear (anxiety, hostility, and guilt) could have provided grist for Dobson's mill. Guilt and anger are treated, but without an adequate biblical foundation.
152.4.D65

Faricy, Robert. *Praying for Inner Healing.*
New York: Paulist Press, 1979.
Part of the growing body of literature
designed to produce a sense of material and
emotional well-being. Helpful. Roman
Catholic. 248.4.F22

Finney, Charles Grandison. *The Promise of
the Spirit.* Compiled and ed. by T. L. Smith.
Minneapolis: Bethany Fellowship, 1980.
Reveals the essence of the holiness teaching which received impetus from Finney's
remarkable ministry. 248.4.F49S 1980

Gaylin, Willard. *Feelings: Our Vital Signs.*
New York: Harper and Row, 1979.
A clear analysis of why we feel the way we
do, how we may attain a better understanding
of our feelings, and how we may turn our
weaknesses into strengths. 152.4.G25

Glasser, William. *Stations of the Mind: New
Directions for Reality Therapy.* New York:
Harper and Row, 1981.
Basing his approach upon Control System
Psychology, Glasser develops a thesis for
behavior control that helps people achieve a
sense of belonging, worth, fun, and freedom.
Provocative. 158.1.G46

Glickman, S. Craig. *Knowing Christ.* Chicago: Moody Press, 1980.
Well-written chapters accurately unfolding
the dynamic of "Christ *in* you, the hope of
glory." Recommended. 248.4.G49

Jourard, Sidney M. *Self-disclosure: An
Experimental Analysis of the Transparent Self.*
Huntington, NY: Robert E. Krieger Publishing Company, 1979.
An analysis of human behavior and the
means of communication, both verbal and
non-verbal, which disclose to others how we
think and feel. Complete with questionnaires,
appendixes, etc. 155.2'8.J83

Kalish, Richard A., and **Kenneth W. Collier.** *Exploring Human Values: Psychological
and Philosophical Considerations.* Monterey,
CA: Brooks/Cole Publishing Company, 1981.
Focusing on personal and social values, the
authors discuss the different philosophical and
psychological issues that undergird human
behavior and mental health. Stimulating
reading. 128.K12

La Haye, Timothy F. *The Battle for the
Mind.* Old Tappan, NJ: Fleming H. Revell
Company, 1980.
Building upon the Scriptural teaching about
the mind, and ably blending this teaching with

an awareness of history and the dangers of
humanism, LaHaye provides his readers with
a positive statement of the blessings and dangers facing each one of us. 211.6.L13

Lee, Francis Nigel. *The Central Significance of Culture.* Nutley, NJ: Presbyterian
and Reformed Publishing Co., 1976.
Contains five lectures and three appendixes. Traces the origin of culture and how
its effects make their impact on society.
Reformed. 301.2.L51

*Lovelace, Richard F. *Dynamics of Spiri-
tual Life: An Evangelical Theology of Renewal.*
Downers Grove, IL: InterVarsity Press, 1979.
Provides a history of spiritual renewal which
isolates doctrinal distinctives from those ele-
ments which produce spiritual growth. Also
deals with the reasons why "revivals" were
shortlived and the results meager. Indexed.
269.2.L94

McKinley, John. *Group Development
Through Participation Training.* New York:
Paulist Press, 1980.
Complete with a "students manual," this
description of groups and the way in which
they work also points the way to mutual
acceptance, support, and growth.
301.1.M21

McMahon, J. J. *Between You and You.* New
York: Paulist Press, 1980.
Dispenses with the traditional approaches
to psychotherapy and concentrates instead
on one's inner thought processes. Enables
readers to "tap into" these concepts and provides guidelines on what to look for. Explains
the significance of one's inner verbalizations,
what they indicate about one's up-and-com-
ing behavior, and what he or she can do about
it. Moderately psychoanalytic. 158.1.M22

Murphey, Cecil. *Prayerobics: Getting
Started and Staying Going.* Waco, TX: Word
Books, 1979.
A practical primer filled with down-to-earth
illustrations and pertinent pointers to improve
the prayer life of the individual, a group, or
the church. 248.3.M95

Nathansen, Bernard N., with **Richard N.
Ostling.** *Aborting America.* Garden City, NY:
Doubleday and Company, 1979.
Reexamines the abortion controversy, the
abortion law, the theories behind the pro-
abortionist lobby, and exposes the flagrant
abuses being practiced in America today.
Highlights the fact that socially this indicates

a diminished respect for human life. Challenging.   301.N19

Needham, David C. *Birthright: Christian Do You Know Who You Are?* Portland, OR: Multnomah Press, 1979.

The author probes the Scriptures with a view to determining a believer's identity—as a person in Christ and as a child of God. Relates the benefits of a Christian's position to sanctification.   248.4.N28

Osborne, Cecil G. *Understanding Your Past, Key to Your Future.* Waco, TX: Word Books, 1980.

While differing in form from Misseldine's *Your Inner Child of the Past*, this work uses some of the same principles as the author spells out his Primal Integration Therapy (PIT). Explains how counselors may tap into the long-suppressed feelings of their counselees.   253.5.0S1P 1980.

Osgood, Donald W. *Pressure Points.* Chappaqua, NY: Christian Herald Books, 1978.

A delightful, practical book outlining in easy-to-read chapters how people can handle stress without coming "unglued." Brings personal self-awareness that results in improved health and enhanced relationships. Highly commended.   248.4.0S3

Owens, Virginia Stem. *The Total Image: Or, Selling Jesus in the Modern Age.* Grand Rapids: Wm. B. Eerdmans Publishing Co., 1980.

A social critique of the use of mass media in the United States for the purpose, ostensibly, of propagating the gospel. Worthy of serious discussion.   269. 2.0W2

Packer, James Innell. *Beyond the Battle for the Bible.* Westchester, IL: Cornerstone Books, 1980.

While not as stimulating as *Knowing God*, this work reminds believers of the importance of Christian *living* if the Gospel is to spread and the world evangelized. Packer's reviews of Berkouwer's *Holy Scripture*, Lindsell's *The Bible in the Balance*, and Rogers and McKim's *Authority and Interpretation of the Bible* are included in an appendix.   248.4.P12

Peterson, Eugene H. *A Long Obedience in the Same Direction: Discipleship in an Instant Society.* Downers Grove, IL: InterVarsity Press, 1980.

A book like this was inevitable. Based primarily on the Book of Psalms, these studies explore personal growth and social problems, and show that progress in Christian life and

service is a long-term project. Valuable for its insights.   248.4.P44

Powell, John. *Unconditional Love.* Niles, IL: Argus Communications, 1978.

Powell states that "there is nothing else that can expand the human soul, actualize the human potential for growth, or bring a person into the full possession of life more than love which is unconditional." He then explains this love in terms of its stages.   248.4.P87

Powers, Bruce P. *Christian Leadership.* Nashville: Broadman Press, 1979.

One of the best works on leadership to appear in recent years. Stresses the importance of the process of leadership rather than the techniques or skills. The valuable principles in this book are, unfortunately, accompanied by inaccuracies in handling Scripture.   158.4.P87

Pierson, Robert H. *How to Become a Successful Christian Leader.* Mountain View, CA: Pacific Press Publishing Association, 1978.

Abounds with practical pointers on how to be more successful in dealing with others. Contains sage counsel for those in the ministry as well.   158.4.P61

Rokeach, Milton. *Understanding Human Values: Individual and Societal.* New York: Free Press, 1979.

In his discussion of desirable core concepts, Rokeach provides an inter-disciplinary evaluation of human values and their place in our everyday lives. An important discussion; abounds in illustrative material. Of real value to the pastor.   301.2'1.R63

Rychlak, Joseph F. *Discovering Free Will and Personal Responsibility.* New York: Oxford University Press, 1979.

Emphasizes the importance of free will in the development of a healthy personality. Explains the areas in which growth may be experienced.   155.2'34.R96

Schaeffer, Francis August, and **C. Everett Koop.** *What Ever Happened to the Human Race?* Old Tappan, NJ: Fleming H. Revell Company, 1979.

Speaks broadly and prophetically about the most serious issues facing the human race— issues reflecting man's inadequacies to cope with the dilemmas he faces.   301.SCH1

*__Stott, John Robert Walmsey.__ *Focus on Christ.* London: Wm. Collins Publishers, 1979.

Eight expository messages stressing the

centrality and sufficiency of Christ in the believer's life and experience. 248.4.S7

*Strauss, Richard L. *Win the Battle for Your Mind*. Wheaton, IL: Victor Books, 1980.

A biblical and theological study of the place and importance of the mind in the life and spiritual growth of the Christian. Also exposes the social forces which, through appeals to the mind and then the senses, seek to conform us to the world's standards and systems of values. 248.27.S8

*Swindoll, Charles Rozell. *Three Steps Forward, Two Steps Back: Persevering Through Pressure*. Nashville: Thomas Nelson Publishers, 1980.

This devotional work is not like other studies dealing with the development of Christian character. In these chapters Swindoll describes typical situations in life and shows how believers may grow by working through their problems. Excellent. 248.4.S6F

Tenney, Merrill Chapin. *Roads a Christian Must Travel: Fresh Insights into the Principles of Christian Experience*. Wheaton, IL: Tyndale House Publishers, 1979.

Takes account of certain journeys mentioned in the NT and gleans from them spiritual principles for believers in their Christian pilgrimage. 248.4.T25

Van Kaam, Adrian. *Living Creatively*. Denville, NJ: Dimension Books, 1972.

Formerly published under the title *Envy and Originality*, this humanistic study centers on the manner in which people may discover their sources of originality and achieve self-motivation. Roman Catholic. 248.4.V32L

――――. *Spirituality and the Gentle Life*. Denville, NJ: Dimension Books, 1974.

A Roman Catholic priest-psychologist discusses one manifestation of the fruit of the Spirit, and in doing so opens up to his readers the facilitating condition embodied in gentleness. Stimulating. 248.4.V32G

Warlick, Harold C., Jr. *Conquering Loneliness*. Waco, TX: Word Books, 1979.

†Based on the Lentz Lectures, Harvard Divinity School. Demonstrates extensive research and an awareness of human needs. Provides important clues on how to help the lonely find meaningful satisfaction in service and in their relationships. 248.48'61.W24

Wessler, Ruth A., and Richard L. Wessler. *The Principles and Practice of Rational-Emotive Therapy*. San Francisco: Jossey-Bass Publishers, 1980.

Analyzes and explains the principles of RET and describes its effectiveness in the client-therapist relationship. 616.89.W51

Whitehead, Evelyn Eaton, and James D. Whitehead. *Christian Life Patterns: The Psychological Challenges and Religious Invitations of Adult Life*. Garden City, NY: Doubleday and Company, 1979.

The authors attempt to reconstruct a contemporary approach to spirituality based upon Eriksonian stages of development. Of value is their discussion of "adult encounters and the often disguised religious invitations" that are present within specific developmental stages. 248.84.W58

Wilson, John Oliver. *After Affluence: Economics to Meet Human Needs*. San Francisco: Harper and Row, 1980.

Tracing the American middle-class dream to the era following World War II, the realization of the value of a good education, and hard work as the means of achieving economic security, Wilson describes the erosion of the dream and the bureaucratic, political, and economic factors affecting our contemporary society. 305.5'5.UN3.W69

Wise, Jonathan Kurland, and Susan Kierr Wise. *The Overeaters: Eating Styles and Personality*. New York: Human Sciences Press, 1979.

The best work to appear on the subject of obesity. Distinguishes between different personality types and shows how these require *different approaches* if the problem is to be corrected. While psychoanalytic, the counsel offered is worthy of serious consideration. Pastoral counselors will find this book well worth the investment. 616.3'98.W75

Chapter 7

MARRIAGE AND FAMILY LIVING

Ackerman, Paul R., and **Murray M. Kappelman.** *Signals: What Your Child Is Really Telling You*. New York: Dial Press, 1978.

Discusses the methods of nonverbal communication used by children—the voiceless "signals" often misinterpreted by parents—and explains their meaning. Also provides suggestions as to how the child's felt needs may be met. 301.42'7.AC5

Alexander, Olive J. *Developing Spiritually Sensitive Children*. Minneapolis: Bethany Fellowship, 1980.

Seeks to pass on to parents the skills by which they may develop a strong internal, and therefore personal, faith in their children. 649'.7.A2

Ames, Louise Bates, et al. *The Gesell Institutes's Child from One to Six: Evaluating the Behavior of the Preschool Child*.

An updated version of the famous work by Gesell, *The First Five Years of Life* (1940), and the equally valuable treatment by Gesell and Ilg of *Child Development* (1949). In this newer work the authors describe for parents the dynamics of physical growth and personality development. Recommended. 155.4'22.G33 1979

————, and **Frances L. Ilg.** *Your Six-Year Old: Defiant but Loving*. New York: Delacorte Press, 1979.

Explores the complex personality of the six-year-old and shows how parents may relate to this loving, yet defiant, member of their family. Excellent. 155.4'24.AM3

————, and **Joan Ames Chase.** *Don't Push Your Preschooler*. Revised ed. New York: Harper and Row, 1980.

This sequel to *School Readiness* and *Stop School Failure* recommends that parents enjoy their children without pushing them to achieve beyond their means. Throughout there is evidence of the author's healthy respect for the individuality of each child. 649'.123.AM3

Arnold, William V. *When Your Parents Divorce*. Philadelphia: Westminster Press, 1980.

Part of a new series of Christian Care Books. Treats the unique problems, feelings of guilt, and special areas of concern experienced by children when their parents separate. Practical and insightful. 301.42'87.AR6

Augsburger, David. *Caring Enough to Confront*. Revised ed. Glendale, CA: Regal Books, 1980.

First published in 1973 under the title *The Love Fight*, this popular work has now been revised. Deserves careful study. 249.AU4 1980

Bakan, David. *And They Took Themselves Wives: The Emergence of Patriarchy in Western Civilization*. San Francisco: Harper and Row, 1979.

†In the wake of social pressures and attacks on traditional marriage customs—challenges that have spawned communes, homosexual marriages and proud unwed mothers—Bakan explores the roots of family solidarity and finds the answer in the patriarchal system of ancient Judaism. 301.42.B17

*Barber, Cyril John, and **Aldyth Ayleen Barber.** *Your Marriage Has Real Possibilities: Biblical Principles for a Successful Marriage*. San Bernardino, CA: Here's Life Publishers, 1980.

Thirteen biblically based studies of marriage and family life which the authors use to develop a model for contemporary Christian couples. Replete with discussion questions. Of value for individual or group Bible study. 249.B23Y

*———, and Gary H. Strauss. *The Effective Parent: Biblical Principles of Parenting Based upon the Model of God the Father.* San Bernardino, CA: Here's Life Publishers, 1980.

Described by Dan Baumann in the foreword as "a happy blend of thoughtfulness and helpfulness . . . ; appeals to both my rationality and my need for a faith that fleshes out in the marketplace." Deals realistically with the practical lessons to be learned from God the Father's handling of Jonah and the Ninevites.   249.B23E

Blackwell, William L., and **Muriel F. Blackwell.** *Working Partners, Working Parents.* Nashville: Broadman Press, 1979.

A social worker and his wife write of the problems which arise when both parents follow their chosen careers. An important contribution.   301.42.B56

Blitchington, W. Peter. *Sex Roles and the Christian Family.* Wheaton, IL: Tyndale House Publishers, 1980.

Written by a Seventh-day Adventist, this capable study probes the natural laws of growth and sexuality, and shows how these contribute to the complexion of the family unit. This book is instructive and may be read with profit by pastoral counselors as well as parents.   301.41.B61

Bridges, William. *Transitions: Making Sense of Life's Changes.* Reading, MA: Addison-Wesley Publishing Company, 1980.

This practical treatise assesses the need for change and identifies the crucial stages of life when such changes take place. Provides counsel on how people may cope "without coming unglued."   303.4.B76

Broderick, Carlfred. *Couples: How to Confront Problems and Maintain Loving Relationships.* New York: Simon and Schuster, 1979.

A leading authority on marriage shares with his readers important principles that will strengthen interpersonal relationships. Recommended. All pastors and counselors should master the contents of this work.

261.42'7.B78C

Bromiley, Geoffrey William. *God and Marriage.* Grand Rapids: Wm. B. Eerdmans Publishing Co., 1980.

Brief and to the point, Bromiley deals with the Trinity and notes how each member of the Godhead affects the marriage of a Christian couple and contributes to its stability.

261.8'358.B78

***Clark, Stephen B.** *Man and Woman in Christ: An Examination of the Roles of Men and Women in Light of Scripture and the Social Sciences.* Ann Arbor, MI: Servant Books, 1980.

A thorough examination of the institution of marriage, the nature of the family, and the roles of husbands and wives, etc. Makes a serious attempt to ground each facet of the study in the Scriptures. Roman Catholic.

261.8'343.C54

Conway, Sally. *You and Your Husband's Mid-Life Crisis.* Elgin, IL: David C. Cook Publishing Co., 1980.

Providing a wife's perspective on the mid-life crisis of her husband, this complement to Jim Conway's *Man in Mid-Life Crisis* describes a wife's experiences and shows other women how to cope with the problems peculiar to this period of life.   612'.665.C76Y

Cully, Iris V. *Christian Child Development.* San Francisco: Harper and Row, 1979.

Applies contemporary psychological research in learning theory to Christian child rearing. Relates the findings of Erikson, Piaget, Kohlberg, etc. to a child's intellectual, emotional, moral, and spiritual development.   268.432.C89C

Dobson, James Clayton, Jr. *Straight Talk to Men and Their Wives.* Waco, TX: Word Books, 1980.

In part a tribute to the author's father, this book concentrates on men. Dobson discusses male identity from both a Christian and a psychological perspective. Of value for men and fathers as well as wives and mothers.

301.4'27.D65S

Dollar, Truman E., and **Grace H. Ketterman.** *Teenage Rebellion.* Old Tappan, NJ: Fleming H. Revell Company, 1980.

Combines an understanding of the psychology of child development with a discussion of the problems of adolescents.

301.43'15.D69

Drakeford, John W. *Marriage: How to Keep a Good Thing Growing.* Nashville: Impact Books, 1979.

Amid the plethora of books on marriage and marital counseling, this one, advocating DMA—Decisive Motivational Action—outlines "action strategies" that are designed to build, and then strengthen, the relationship of the couple. Behavioral; of real value to pastoral counselors.   249.D78

Drescher, John M. *What Should Parents Expect?* Nashville: Abingdon Press, 1980.
Covers the stages of child development and offers pointers as to the way in which parents may instill moral values in their sons and daughters. 261.8'342.D81

Ellison, Craig W. *Loneliness: The Search for Intimacy.* Chappaqua, NY: Christian Herald Press, 1980.
Directs the attention of readers to one of the leading problems of our age; ably correlates biblical teaching on the subject with the latest psychological research; and provides perceptive guidelines which pastors and counselors will find helpful. 248.8'6.EL5

Freeman, Carroll B. *The Senior Adult Years: A Christian Psychology of Aging.* Nashville: Broadman Press, 1979.
Comprehensive and complete, this work exhibits an understanding of the problems of the aged and provides guidelines so that those who work with them may make their declining years fulfilling. Recommended.
155.67.F87

Getz, Gene A. *The Measure of a Marriage.* Glendale, CA: Regal Books, 1980.
Packed with practical information, outlines, and exercises, this handy book can be read with profit by all who are married or who contemplate marriage. 301.42.G33

Gottman, John Mordecai. *Marital Interaction: Experimental Investigations.* New York: Academic Press, 1979.
The English-speaking world has come to respect the writings of this esteemed social psychologist. In this work he discusses the results of his research into contemporary forms of marital communication—with some interesting discoveries. Pastors may validly apply the truths Gottman uncovers to the needs of some of the those in their congregation. 301.42.G71M

Gundry, Patricia. *The Complete Woman.* Garden City, NY: Doubleday and Company, 1981.
Having suffered much for her beliefs in the equality of men and women, though refusing all identification with "Women's Lib" and the ERA, Gundry here expounds on Proverbs 31 and, with material relevant to the needs of those of her sex, establishes a biblical basis for womanhood in our contemporary society. Excellent. 301.41.G95C

_____. *Heirs Together.* Grand Rapids: Zondervan Publishing House, 1980.
A courageous description of marriage, its privileges, limitations, and reciprocal responsibilities, with a logical, balanced discussion of mutual submission. 249.G95H

Halverson, Kaye, with **Karen M. Hess.** *The Wedded Unmother.* Minneapolis: Augsburg Publishing House, 1980.
A sympathetic discussion of the plight of the childless wife. Shares her hurts and provides comforting counsel for those trying to overcome infertility. 301.42.H16

Hancock, Maxine. *The Forever Principle.* Old Tappan, NJ: Fleming H. Revell Company, 1980.
Develops a persuasive apologetic for a firm commitment on the part of those entering into marriage. Describes the benefits which accrue to the couple and the way in which such a commitment forms a basis for all work toward meaningful solutions to interpersonal problems and satisfaction in marriage.
301.42.H19

Harcum, Eugene Rae. *Psychology for Daily Living: Simple Guidance in Human Relations for Parents, Teachers, and Others.* Chicago: Nelson-Hall, 1979.
Describes the basics of human behavior—the kinds of reactions to problems and situations which characterize different kinds of people. Can readily be understood by the average reader. 158.H21

Hass, Aaron. *Teenage Sexuality: A Survey of Teenage Sexual Behavior.* New York: Macmillan Publishing Company, 1979.
A recent and, from all accounts, reliable assessment of teenage sexual mores. Based upon extensive experiential research. Makes sobering reading, particularly when pastors realize that young people within the church are exposed to peer pressure which often results in the kind of behavior described in this book. 301.41'75.H27

Hendricks, Jeanne W. *Afternoon: For Women at the Heart of Life.* Nashville: Thomas Nelson Publishers, 1979.
Directing the attention of her readers to "the most joyful, the most productive, the most leisurely years of a woman's life," Mrs. Hendricks discusses the challenges of "midlife crisis" and shows how, by investing oneself in people, the "afternoon" of life can be rewarding and fulfilling. 248'.843.H38

Heim, Pamela. *The Art of Married Love.* Irvine, CA: Harvest House Publishers, 1978.

Imperfect people make imperfect spouses and have imperfect marriages. This book shows how a couple may create a harmonious atmosphere in which to work on their respective failings.					249.H36

Henslin, James M., ed. *Marriage and Family in a Changing Society.* New York: The Free Press, 1980.

In 42 brief chapters the contributors discuss all aspects of the interpersonal process from premarital courtship and the romantic ideal to marital adjustments and the future of the family.					301.42.H39

Herron, Orley. *Who Controls Your Child?* Nashville: Thomas Nelson Publishers, 1980.

Sobering in his revelation of the destructive forces surrounding children and youth today, Herron nevertheless is able to challenge parents with a realistic plan of action. He shows them how the home may constructively offset the impact of our social milieu. A must for all parents.					649'.1.H43

*Hindson, Edward E.** *The Total Family.* Wheaton, IL: Tyndale House Publishers, 1980.

Drawing information from many sources, Hindson integrates his material with the Scriptures and presents to his readers practical guidelines for all members of the family.					301.4.H58

Holmes, Deborah Lott, and **Frederick J. Morrison.** *The Child: An Introduction to Developmental Psychology.* Monterey, CA: Brooks/Cole Publishing Co., 1979.

Assists the busy pastor in keeping pace with the changes which have taken place during the past twenty years, knowing how to respond to cases of child abuse, being able to counsel those in the church's educational program on how to relate to, encourage, and instruct children in accordance with their growth. Provides timely help for young parents. Excellent.					155.4.H73

Jensen, Gordon D. *Youth and Sex: Pleasure and Responsibility.* 2d ed. Chicago: Nelson-Hall, 1979.

Written for teenagers by a medical doctor, this book treats such topics as masturbation, petting, sexual intercourse, venereal disease, etc. Secular.					170.1.J45

*Johnston, Olaf Raymond.** *Who Needs the Family?* Downers Grove, IL: InterVarsity Press, 1979.

Biblically and sociologically sound, this astute discussion of changes taking place in modern marriages not only assesses the past but points the way to reconstruction so that our children may have a viable future.					301.4.J64

Kasper, Walter. *Theology of Christian Marriage.* New York: Seabury Press, 1980.

†Having set the Scriptures aside as normative, Kasper attempts to reconstruct from historical research what social groups through the centuries have thought about marriage and how social mores have brought it to its present state of evolution.					261.8'34.K15

Kelly, Robert K. *Courtship, Marriage, and the Family.* 3d ed. New York: Harcourt, Brace and Jovanovich, 1979.

A complete coverage of marriage from patterns of courtship to old age. Includes important chapters on pairing, the problems of premarital relations, changing roles, marriage expectations, dual careers, sexual adjustment, the place of religion, children or childlessness, adoption, etc. Ideal for those who work with young people and couples in the church.					301.42.K28 1979.

Kendall, Earline Doak, and **Betty Doak Elder.** *Train Up Your Child . . . A Guide for Christian Parents.* Nashville: Abingdon Press, 1980.

A brother and sister, both married with families of their own, team up to write on the importance of nurturing children in the way of the Lord. In a series of important chapters they describe the process, the problems, and the rewards.					649.7.K33

Klimek, David. *Beneath Mate Selection and Marriage: The Unconscious Motives in Human Pairing.* New York: Van Nostrand Reinhold Company, 1979.

This helpful manual will be welcomed by all youth pastors and those involved in premarital counseling. It describes the maturation process and the origin of character traits which lead young people to instinctively select a certain type of spouse, frequently with unhappy results. The careful study of this work will be of particular value to those interested in preventing problems from arising, rather than seeking to remedy them after they develop.					301.41'43.K68

Knight, Bryan M. *Enjoying Single Parenthood.* New York: Van Nostrand Reinhold, 1980.

Deals with a wide variety of single-parent situations and experiences. Provides practical guidance and a positive approach for this growing segment of American society. Good principles can be culled from this book without adopting its seemingly permissive morality.   362.8'2.K74

Lamm, Maurice. *The Jewish Way in Love and Marriage.* San Francisco: Harper and Row, 1980.

While not of the order of Neufeld's *Ancient Hebrew Marriage Laws* or Epstein's numerous works on Jewish marriage customs, this excellent treatment of the history, traditions, and practices associated with Jewish marital rites meets a felt need and provides valuable insights.   301.42.L18

Lee, Mark W. *How to Have a Good Marriage Before and After the Wedding.* Chappaqua, New York: Christian Herald Books, 1978.

The bulk of this book consists of fifty questions and answers which the author believes will prepare a couple for marriage.
301.42.L51H

Lewis, Margaret M., with **Gregg A. Lewis.** *The Hurting Parent.* Grand Rapids: Zondervan Publishing House, 1980.

This mother-son team writes emphatically of the problems of child-rearing and the difference a vital Godward relationship can make. A *must* for every church library.
248.8'6.L58

Linthorst, Ann Tremaine. *A Gift of Love: Marriage as a Spiritual Journey.* New York: Paulist Press, 1979.

Written by a marriage and family counselor, this treatment covers both old and new ground. It reasserts some long-held, basic beliefs about marriage and applies spiritual principles to the everyday problems married couples encounter.   249.L65

Ludwig, David J. *The Spirit of Your Marriage.* Minneapolis: Augsburg Publishing House, 1979.

Describes ways in which Christian couples can create a richer and more fulfilling environment for the cultivation of their marital relationship.   301.42.L96

Mattson, Lloyd, and **Elsie Mattson.** *Rediscover Your Family Outdoors.* Wheaton, IL: Victor Books, 1980.

A reminder of the ways in which families may achieve a sense of togetherness through one-day excursions from the home, travel, hiking, and camping. Practical.
796.54.M43R

Mayfield, James L. *Up with Marriage: A Positive Adventure in Marriage Enrichment Through Improved Communication.* Independence, MO: Herald Publishing House, 1979.

The author places his finger on the #1 cause of marital breakdown. Describes the steps which couples can take in order to clear the channels of communication.   301.42.M45

Meier, Paul D., and **Linda Burnett.** *The Unwanted Generation: A Guide to Responsible Parenting.* Grand Rapids: Baker Book House, 1980.

Consists of reciprocal statements by a Christian psychiatrist and a young Christian mother on key issues facing parents.
301.43.M48

————, and **Richard Meier.** *Family Foundations: How to Have a Happy Home.* Grand Rapids: Baker Book House, 1981.

Describes the ups and downs of contemporary marriages and shows how a solid biblical foundation can help ease some of the hurts and iron out some of the wrinkles.
301.4.M47

Meredith, Donald. *Becoming One.* Nashville: Thomas Nelson Publishers, 1979.

Treats objectively five common pitfalls of marriage and explains in clear, concise terms what Christian couples can do to strengthen their union. Concludes with a section containing practical counsel on role relationships, sex, finances, etc. A handy book to give to courting couples.   301.42.M54

Minirth, Frank, et al. *The Workaholic and His Family: An Inside Look.* Grand Rapids: Baker Book House, 1981.

Traces the workaholic's compulsion to feelings of guilt, describes the effect of his habits on his family, and points the way to recovery. Practical.   152.442.M66

Mussen, Paul Henry; John Janeway Conger; and Jerome Kagan. *Child Development and Personality.* 5th ed. New York: Harper and Row, 1979.

With the attention of parents, pastors, and teachers focusing more and more on the importance of proper child development, this welcome text condenses into a single volume a wealth of practical material. Well indexed.
155.4'18.M97 1979.

Narramore, Stanley Bruce. *Adolescence Is Not An Illness.* Old Tappan, NJ: Fleming H. Revell Company, 1980.

Deals with the fluctuating moods and problems of adolescents, and offers parents creative alternatives to teenage negativism, peer pressures, discipline, etc.   305.2'3.N16

_____. *Why Children Misbehave.* Grand Rapids: Zondervan Publishing House, 1980.
Counsels parents on how to prevent problems from arising on the lives of their children. Describes the causes of bad behavior and directs parents on how to implement change.   649'.1.N16W

Plekker, Robert J. *Divorce and the Christian: What the Bible Teaches.* Wheaton, IL: Tyndale House Publishers, 1980.
A compassionate discussion which grapples with the hard questions and ably applies biblical truth to life's questions. A good book to place in the church library.   173.1.P71

Rice, David G. *Dual-Career Marriage: Conflict and Treatment.* New York: Free Press, 1979.
With the virtual disappearance of the nuclear family and the emergence of a group who wish to be more than working wives, a book such as this one becomes essential. In nontechnical terms, Rice discusses the problems, trade-offs, pitfalls, and potential of this new phenomenon.   301.42.R36

*Richards, Lawrence O.**, and **Paul Johnson.** *Death and the Caring Community, Ministering to the Terminally Ill.* Portland, OR: Multnomah Press, 1980.
An excellent statement of the needs of the community and the response of those who can comprise the caring nucleus of the church. Should be mandatory reading in all seminaries.   259.4.R39

Roberts, Betty Holroyd. *Middle-Aged Career Dropouts.* Cambridge, MA: Schenkman Publishing Company, 1980.
Part of the growing plethora of books providing readers with an understanding of the problems of the middle-aged.   301.5'5.R54

Robinson, James. *In Search of a Father.* Life's Answer Series. Wheaton, IL: Tyndale House Publishers, 1980.
Zeroes in on fatherhood. Describes what fathers should be like and what their children expect of them.   301.421'2.R56

_____, with **Jimmie Cox.** *The Right Mate.* Wheaton, IL: Tyndale House Publishers, 1979.
Designed for teenagers, this oversimplified book on love, dating, and marriage is designed to help those who think they are "in love" discern between sentimentality and *agape*

love, and prepare themselves for the future.   301.421.R56

Roleder, George. *Marriage Means Encounter.* 2d ed. Dubuque, IA: Wm. C. Brown Company Publishers, 1979.
An anthology of articles from a wide variety of sources. Explores the alternatives to marriage and then focuses on the problems married couples face.   301.42.R64

Rowatt, G. Wade, and **Mary Jo Rowatt.** *The Two-Career Marriage.* Philadelphia: Westminster Press, 1980.
In the wake of the demise of the nuclear family and the emergence of dual-career families, this practical book zeroes in on the problems created and provides guidelines on how to handle the pressures that will be experienced by the couple.   306.8.R78

Rubin, Lillian B. *Women of a Certain Age: The Middle Search for Self.* New York: Harper and Row, 1979.
While non-Christian in orientation, this work can assist women to understand their "mid-life crisis." It also provides insights for pastors and counselors who need to continue to minister to them as members of the church.   301.43'4.R82

Saul, Leon J. *The Childhood Emotional Pattern and Maturity.* New York: Van Nostrand Reinhold Company, 1979.
This, Saul's twelfth book on personality development, points out that emotional maturity is the key to a happy, meaningful life. In order to apply this theory to child development, Saul explains how fight-flight reaction, feelings of inferiority, and other traits are developed—and how, through an emotionally unhealthy childhood, neurotic tendencies can be developed. Secular.   155.4'18.S8

_____. *The Childhood Emotional Pattern in Marriage.* New York: Van Nostrand Reinhold Company, 1979.
A companion volume to *The Childhood Emotional Pattern and Maturity*, this study takes the author's research a step further and, on the one hand, explains why the divorce-to-marriage ratio is so high, and on the other, offers practical guidelines on how parents may prepare their children for marriage. A valuable resource tool for counselors too.   301.422.S8

Schwartz, Roslyn, and **Leonard J. Schwartz.** *Becoming a Couple.* Englewood Cliffs, NJ: Prentice-Hall, 1980.
While there is nothing new about this sub-

ject, this couple, a psychotherapist and a psychologist respectively, explore the dynamics of interpersonal relationships from dating through marriage to the rearing of children and old age. Insightful.   306.8.SCH9

Sharma, Prakash C. *Aging and Communications: A Selected Bibliographic Research Guide.* Monticello, IL: Vance Bibliographies, 1978.
A handy volume for all who work with the elderly. Should provide ideas for more than one D.Min. dissertation.
                                    016.301.SH2 1978

Simons, Joseph. *Living Together: Communication to the Unmarried Relationship.* Chicago: Nelson-Hall, 1978.
Probes the reasons why young people and others choose to live together. Includes a discussion of the repression of feelings, fear, insecurity, jealousy, anger, etc. Provides insights which pastors and counselors will find helpful.   301.11.S5

Slonaker, David F. *Teenagers Ahead.* Chicago: Nelson-Hall, 1980.
Written for parents, this practical primer contains pointers showing how parents may relate to their children, keep open the lines of communication, and allow them freedom to make decisions, accept responsibility, stress the positive in their lives and relationships, and grow toward maturity.   649.1.S5

Small, Dwight Hervey. *How Should I Love You?* San Francisco: Harper and Row, 1979.
This indispensable work ably distinguishes between infatuation and love, romance and caring. Corrects the emphasis in today's society which mistakenly stresses the ephemeral and the sensational, leaving young people and their elders to flounder through marriage, vainly expecting their experience to square with their misguided ideals. Recommended.   249.SM1H

Smith, Harold Ivan. *A Part of Me Is Missing.* Irvine, CA: Harvest House Publishers, 1979.
Printed on newsprint paper, this "handbook" addresses itself to the needs of an evergrowing group of Americans—8.1 million at last count—who have been divorced and have not married. It also provides practical pointers for those in the church, demonstrating how they can minister to this important segment of society.   301.428'4.S5

Spray, Pauline E. *The Autumn Years: How to Approach Retirement.* Kansas City, MO: Beacon Hill Press, 1979.

A practical guidebook for those approaching their retirement; will be appreciated by those who work with the aged. Shows how the life of the aged can be filled with fun and meaning.   301.435.S7

Stinett, Nick; **Barbara Chesser,** and **John De Fain.** *Building Family Strengths: Blueprints for Action.* Lincoln, NE: University of Nebraska Press, 1979.
Dealing with "Perspectives on Family Strengths," "Family Enrichment and Counseling," "Strengthening Families Through More Effective Parenting," "Parenting Children with Special Needs," "Emerging Family Styles," etc., this symposium contains a wealth of information which those who minister to families will find usable. Secular.
                                    301.421.B86S

Stollak, Gary E. *Until We Are Six: Toward the Actualization of Our Children's Human Potential.* Huntington, NY: Robert E. Krieger Publishing Company, 1978.
A most important work for all who are engaged in the vital task of rearing their children during their most formative years.
                                    155.4.S6

*****Swindoll, Charles Rozell.** *Home, Where Life Makes Up Its Mind.* Portland, OR: Multnomah Press, 1979.
Beautifully written chapters which zero in on the pressure points of contemporary family living. Perceptive.   248.4.S6H

*_____. *Strike the Original Match.* Portland, OR: Multnomah Press, 1980.
Prophet-like in his call to return to biblical principles, Swindoll exposes the fallacious thinking of the times and challenges Christians with the responsibilities and privileges of marriage. Recommended.
                                    301.42.S6 (Alt. DDC 249)

Thatcher, Floyd, and **Harriett Thatcher.** *Long Term Marriage: A Search for the Ingredients of a Lifetime Partnership.* Waco, TX: Word Books, 1980.
Following careful research, the Thatchers provide pointers which couples can adopt and apply to their own relationships. Assists husbands and wives in developing realistic expectations, enhancing their commitment to one another, using conflict to strengthen their marriage, etc. Eminently practical. Recommended.   301.42.T32

Thomas, David M. *Family Life and the Church.* New York: Paulist Press, 1979.

Written by a Roman Catholic, this brief book deals with the basic issues which undergird all marital relationships. Provides practical insights that should help most couples.
249.T36

Travis, Patricia Y., and **Robert P. Travis.** *Vitalizing Intimacy in Marriage (VIM).* Chicago: Nelson-Hall, 1979.
Succeeds in spelling out how couples who really want to can put vitality back into their marital relationship. Emphasizes the prevention of problems rather than their cure.
301.42.T69

Tufte, Virginia, and **Barbara Myerhoff**, eds. *Changing Images of the Family.* New Haven, CT: Yale University Press, 1979
In this book the authors discuss comprehensively and yet concisely the social pressures and practical tensions being experienced by families today. Includes discussion of the influence of literature, art, and the mass media on the family.   301.42'09.C36 1979.

Vernon, Robert, and **C. C. Carlson.** *The Married Man.* Old Tappan, NJ: Fleming H. Revell Company, 1980.
Written by the Assistant Chief of Police, Los Angeles, this book outlines the servant leadership of the husband and father as he fulfills the roles of family head and chief communicator. Practical.   155.6.V58

Voshell, Dorothy. *Whom Shall I Marry? A Question of Vital Concern to Young Chris-*

tians, Their Parents and the Church. Phillipsburg, NJ: Presbyterian and Reformed Publishing Co., 1979.
A careful delineation of the consequences of one's marriage for oneself, one's children, and one's church.   301.41.V92

Ward, Ted. *Values Begin at Home.* Wheaton, IL: Victor Books, 1979.
Ideal for adult discussion groups, this work by an educator and father lays down solid principles for the inculcation of moral values in children. Excellent.   301.21.W21

Warren, Thomas B., ed. *Your Marriage Can Be Great! . . .* Jonesboro, AR: National Christian Press, 1978.
A symposium of 97 chapters by 61 writers, treating the major areas of marriage and family living. Biblically based, each of the twelve major sections deals with aspects of counseling pastors encounter continually. While most of the contributors are associated with the Church of Christ, this work can be read with profit by all engaged in ministering to families.   301.42.W25

Wright, Harry Norman, and **Marvin N. Inmon.** *Preparing For Parenthood.* Ventura, CA: Regal Books, 1980.
Brief but forthright chapters on the issues surrounding parenthood, the expectations of the expectant parents, and the best ways to prepare for the arrival of a new member of the family.   301.426.W93

Chapter 8

PASTORAL THEOLOGY

General Works

Adams, Jay Edward. *Shepherding God's Flock: A Preacher's Handbook on Pastoral Ministry, Counseling, and Leadership.* Grand Rapids: Baker Book House, 1979.

The reissue in one volume of three books in this series. Originally published between 1974-75.   251.AD1S 1979.

Armstrong, Ben. *The Electric Church.* Nashville: Thomas Nelson and Son, 1979.

Surveys the origins and development of religious radio and television. Discusses the problems raised by the widespread use of media and its impact on the future.
      253.7'8.AR5

Banks, Robert. *Paul's Idea of Community: The Early House Churches in Their Historical Setting.* Grand Rapids: Wm. B. Eerdmans Publishing Co., 1980.

Correlates Paul's method of establishing churches with the teaching of the NT. Ably delineates between different kinds of churches and avoids the extremes between legalistic churches and those that are more permissive.
      262.B22

Bromiley, Geoffrey William. *Children of Promise: The Case for Baptizing Infants.* Grand Rapids: Wm. B. Eerdmans Publishing Co., 1979.

An articulate defense of infant baptism in which the author combines history with theology in order to establish a basis in covenant theology for pedo-baptism.   265.12.B78

Criswell, Wallie Amos. *Criswell's Guidebook for Pastors.* Nashville: Broadman Press, 1980.

This compendium of pastoral counsel provides pithy comments on virtually every aspect of the ministry: the preacher's call, his rewards, preparation for the pulpit, the administration of ceremonies and ordinances, staff relations, combating discouragement, etc.
      253.C86 1980

Davis, James Hill, and **Woodie W. White.** *Racial Transition in the Church.* Nashville: Abingdon Press, 1980.

Produced by two leaders of the United Methodist Church, this work documents six years of extensive research in most of the major metropolitan areas in the U.S. Records changes within society and the problems attending integration. Well done.   261.8.D29

*****Engel, James F.** *Contemporary Christian Communications: Its Theory and Practice.* Nashville: Thomas Nelson Publishers, 1979.

This book meets a very real need in that it distinguishes between witnessing and evangelism, and shows how both may become an integral part of a believer's lifestyle. Applies the basic principles of communication to people in all areas of the ministry. Recommended.   253.7.EN3

*****Gallup, George, Jr.**, and **David Poling.** *The Search for America's Faith.* Nashville: Abingdon Press, 1980.

An epochal work which probes the attitudes, needs, and desires of youth, the family, different religious groups, the church, the validity of religious experience, and prospects for the future. Points to the needs of the hour. Should be read by all in the ministry.
      209'.73.G13

Girard, Robert C. *Brethren, Hang Together: Restructuring the Church for Relationships.* Grand Rapids: Zondervan Publishing House, 1979.

This sequel to *Brethren, Hang Loose* advocates and applies the principles of the relational revolution to the church. In contrast to other books of this nature, Girard does attempt to maintain a solid theological foundation while providing pointers that show how loving concern can be developed within the community.   262'.001.G44 T

Hale, James Russell. *The Unchurched: Who They Are and Why They Stay Away.* San Fran-

cisco: Harper and Row, 1980.
Following extensive interviews, the author analyzes in a tenfold way the causes which keep many people away from church. Illuminating.   306.6.H13

Hesselgrave, David J. *Planting Churches Cross Culturally: A Guide for Home and Foreign Missions.* Grand Rapids: Baker Book House, 1980.
This wide-ranging book on the theory, theology, methodology, and history of missions explains each facet of cross-cultural communication in the missionary enterprise. Recommended.   266'.001.H46

Hiltner, Seward. *The Christian Shepherd: Some Aspects of Pastoral Care.* Nashville: Abingdon Press, 1980.
First published in 1959, this pioneer work in the field of modern pastoral theory and practice remains one of the most innovative and helpful works ever written.
253.H56 1980.

Irion, Paul E. *The Funeral and the Mourners: Pastoral Care of the Bereaved.* Nashville: Abingdon Press, 1979.
This book first appeared a quarter of a century ago. It is a complete, helpful, and sound introduction to the funeral, from first telephone call to follow-up counseling. Contains an excellent discussion of the psychology of grief.   253.5.IR4

McGavran, Donald Anderson, and **George G. Hunter, III.** *Church Growth: Strategies That Work.* Nashville: Abingdon Press, 1980.
Emphasizes the ways in which each local assembly can realize maximum outreach via the principles of church growth. Practical, informative, stimulating.   254.5.M17C 1980.

Martin, Ralph Philip. *The Family and the Fellowship: New Testament Images of the Church.* Grand Rapids: Wm. B. Eerdmans Publishing Co., 1979.
Purports to be an explanation of *koinonia* for church members. Unfortunately, the reader may get lost in a maze of questionable textual- and higher-critical theories. For discerning readers only.   262.7.M36

Mylander, Charles. *Secrets for Growing Churches.* San Francisco: Harper and Row, 1979.
In five tightly-packed chapters, the author applies the principles of church growth to congregational renewal. The insights provided in this book will undoubtedly prove useful to pastors.   254.5.M99

*Pickering, Ernest. *Biblical Separation: The Struggle for a Pure Church.* Schaumburg, IL: Regular Baptist Press, 1979.
Well-outlined and well-documented, this biblically based study demonstrates conclusively the imperative necessity of doctrinal purity and holiness of life if the church is to have an effective ministry to the world.
262.P58

Raines, Robert A. *New Life in the Church.* Revised ed. San Francisco: Harper and Row, 1980.
Emphasizing a relational approach to the ministry of the church, Raines describes the benefits and impact of small groups in the church.   253.7.R13

*Rayburn, Robert G. *O Come, Let Us Worship: Corporate Worship in the Evangelical Church.* Grand Rapids: Baker Book House, 1980.
Forcefully confronts Christians with the importance of and need for true worship. Supplies guidelines showing how the neglect of this important activity may be remedied.
264.R21

Stedman, Ray C. *Body Life.* Glendale, CA: Regal Books, 1979.
The reissue of this famous work in an enlarged format.   264.ST3 1979

Walrath, Douglas Alan. *Leading Churches Through Change.* Nashville: Abingdon Press, 1979.
Contains important case studies of churches confronted with the inevitability of change.
254.5.W16

*Warns, Johannes. *Baptism: Studies in the Original Christian Baptism, Its History and Conflicts, . . .* Translated by G. H. Lang. Minneapolis: Klock and Klock Christian Publishers, 1980.
Reprinted from the 1957 edition published in England, this thorough apologetic for believer's baptism evidences a remarkable mastery of philosophy and history, diverse ecclesiastical practices, and theology. Practical, relevant, written with conviction.
265.13.W24 1980.

Watson, David. *I Believe in the Church.* Grand Rapids: Wm. B. Eerdmans Publishing Co., 1979.
Written by an Episcopalian, this popular yet substantive work covers all the major facets of the church, including its purpose and ministry. Inspirational.   262.W33.

Wilke, Harold H. *Creating a Caring Congregation.* Nashville: Abingdon Press, 1980.

The subtitle on the cover captures the theme of this book: *"Guidelines for Ministering with* [not to] *the Handicapped."* The author, an M.D., treats the special needs of the handicapped and the ways in which unconditional love and acceptance may be shown them.
261.8'324.W65.

*****Woodbridge, John D.**; **Mark A. Noll**; and **Nathan O. Hatch.** *The Gospel in America: Themes in the Story of America's Evangeli-* *cals.* Grand Rapids: Zondervan Publishing House, 1979.

Retraces American religious history, showing how, through the ministry of great men of God as well as through a variety of political figures, the movements and events which have transpired have been related to religious experience. Describes the numerous "turning points" which have either instilled a greater God-consciousness in people, or caused them to depart from Him. Recommended.
269.2.AM3.W85.

Pastoralia

Bailey, Robert W., and **Mary Frances Bailey.** *Coping with Stress in the Minister's Home.* Nashville: Broadman Press, 1979.

Without complaint or criticism the authors treat the peculiar pressures of the pastor's wife and deal practically with the physical, emotional, and social issues she faces, offering some guidelines whereby the minister's family can creatively cope with stress.
253.2.B15.

Brekke, Milo L.; **Merton P. Strommen**; and **Dorothy L. Williams.** *Ten Faces of Ministry: Perspectives on Pastoral and Congregational Effectiveness Based on a Survey of 5000 Lutherans.* Minneapolis: Augsburg Publishing House, 1979.

Based upon extensive research, the message of this book extends beyond the boundaries of the three Lutheran church bodies who sponsored the survey. The findings contain some dos and don'ts for pastors that they will do well to heed. Excellent. 253.B74

Career Guide to Professional Associations: A Directory of Organizations by Occupational Field. Cranston, RI: Carroll Press, 1980.

Compiled and edited by the staff of Carroll Press, this detailed alphabetical directory of organizations provides, in addition to the name, address, and telephone number of each organization, a note on the purpose of the organization, date of founding, membership numbers and requirements, frequency of meetings, titles of publications, career fields represented, and career aids offered. Includes a brief description of the major occupational classifications as they are defined in the *Dictionary of Occupational Titles*. The classification of all organizations by occupational field follows this introduction to the *D.O.T.* system. Organizations are listed under each classification in which they are active.
262.2.C18.

Dittes, James E. *When People Say No: Conflict and the Call to the Ministry.* New York: Harper and Row, 1979.

Tackles the hard questions of what a minister is to do when confronted by opposition from the congregation he serves. Shows how such frustrations may be the beginning of a healthy interrelationship. 253.D63.

Driggers, B. Carlisle. *Models of Metropolitan Ministry: How Twenty Churches Are Ministering Successfully in Areas of Rapid Change.* Nashville: Broadman Press, 1979.

This compilation of case studies of twenty churches from across the U.S. pinpoints the ways in which they are coping with change. Includes examples of central city, inner city, suburban, and rural-urban churches. Ecumenical. 254.22.M72.

Hiltner, Seward. *Preface to Pastoral Theology.* Nashville: Abingdon Press, 1979.

†First published in 1958, this book created a new trend in practical theology. Makes a strong case for including this discipline under theology and stresses the importance of the "shepherding" role of the pastor.
250.SH4.H56 1979.

Mace, David Robert, and **Vera Mace.** *What's Happening to Clergy Marriages?* Nashville: Abingdon Press, 1980.

Discusses the occupational hazards of the ministry and shows how the pressures generated can lead to breakdown in one's marriage. A welcome treatise which treats fairly a long-neglected aspect of the ministry.
248.4.M26W.

Olson, Robert Wallace. *The Art of Creative Thinking.* New York: Barnes and Noble Books, 1980.

Not since Osborne's *Applied Imagination* (1963) has a work as practical as this one been published. Olson shows how to cultivate one's imagination and then put his newly acquired skills to good use. 153.3'5.0L8.

Ross, Charlotte. *Who is the Minister's Wife? A Search for Personal Fulfillment.* Philadelphia: Westminster Press, 1980.

This excellent little treatise is *must* reading for pastors' wives, and should be required

reading for all studying for the ministry. Its practical approach and sane counsel bring into focus the unique pressures and problems of those called to help their husbands in the work of the Lord. Excellent. 253.2.R73.

Turnbull, Ralph G. *A Minister's Opportunities.* Grand Rapids: Baker Book House, 1979.

This companion volume to *The Minister's Obstacles* challenges each pastor with the possibility of becoming all that God meant him to be. It is a down-to-earth, practical book containing sage advice from a senior minister. 253.2.T84M.

Evangelism

Dayton, Edward R. *That Everyone May Hear: Reaching the Unreached.* Monrovia, CA: MARC, 1979.

This special edition of a well-received work illustrates how Christians may reach out and evangelize others. 269.2.D33T.

———, and David Allen Fraser. *Planning Strategies for World Evangelization.* Grand Rapids: Wm. B. Eerdmans Publishing Co., 1980.

A comprehensive consideration of the issues and alternatives facing evangelicals in missions today. Recommended. 266.D33P.

Eichhorn, David Max. *Evangelizing the American Jew.* Middle Village, NJ: Jonathan David, 1978.

Deals with the history of Christian attempts to convert Jews to Hebrew Christianity and Messianic Judaism. 253.7.EI2.

*Getz, Gene A.** *Loving One Another.* Wheaton, IL: Victor Books, 1979.

Lays a secure foundation for an evangelistic lifestyle. Discusses the concept of discipleship within the context of a willingness to serve one another. Corrects many of our earlier false impressions about evangelism. Timely. 260.G33L.

Hoekstra, Harvey Thomas. *The World Council of Churches and the Demise of Evangelism.* Wheaton, IL: Tyndale House Publishers, 1979.

Well-documented and insightful, this historico-theological analysis of the missionary activity of the WCC traces the movement from 1910 to 1975. Of value is the author's exposé of the subtle ways in which, over the years,

the WCC has turned attention away from world evangelism to social involvement which in some instances borders on Marxism. Highly readable. 262'.001.H67.

Johnston, Robert K. *Evangelicals at an Impasse.* Atlanta: John Knox Press, 1979.

Assesses the major issues facing the church today: inerrancy, the role of women, homosexuality, social ethics, etc. Critical of evangelicals, but has words of praise for those who have redefined inerrancy, such as D. A. Hubbard and C. H. Pinnock. While interesting, this work may be welcomed only by those advocating theological compromise. 261.8.J64.

Korthals, Richard G. *Agape Evangelism: Roots That Reach Out.* Wheaton, IL: Tyndale House Publishers, 1980.

Korthals explores the motives for, as well as the means of, evangelism. Rooted firmly in the NT. A valuable supplement to Chafer's *True Evangelism: Winning Souls by Prayer.* Emphasizes the relational aspect of ministering out of a heart overflowing with God's love. 269.2.K84.

Lindgren, Alvin J., and **Norman Shawchuck.** *Let My People Go: Empowering Laity for Ministry.* Nashville: Abingdon Press, 1980.

Well reasoned and "on target," this discussion of the potential of laypeople comes likes a breath of fresh air to those engaged in the ministry. 253.L64L.

McDill, Wayne. *Making Friends for Christ.* Nashville: Broadman Press, 1979.

Capitalizes on human need for relationship and shows how believers may use their homes or other means to establish friendships with a view to winning people to Christ.

248.5.M14

Pippert, Rebecca Manley. *Out of the Salt-Shaker and Into the World: Evangelism as a Way of Life.* Downers Grove, IL: InterVarsity Press, 1979.

Twelve well-written chapters in true IVCF style. Designed to defuse the reader's anxiety over witnessing.   269.2.P66

*Richards, Lawrence O. *Sixty-Nine Ways to Start a Study Group and Keep it Growing.* Grand Rapids: Zondervan Publishing House, 1980.

First published in 1973, this important "how-to" manual focuses on the people as well as the purpose of Bible study groups. A *must.*   269.2.R39

White, James F. *Introduction to Christian Worship.* Nashville: Abingdon Press, 1980.

This treatment of liturgics deals with historical and theological dimensions of sacramentalism and then describes how a pastor may encourage real worship in the church. Ecumenical.   264.W58

Wilson, J. Christy, Jr. *Today's Tentmakers: Self-support—An Alternative Model for Worldwide Witness.* Wheaton, IL: Tyndale House Publishers, 1979.

An answer to the inflationary costs of missions, this innovative book explains how Christians may effectively witness for Christ at home and abroad while supporting themselves as did the apostle Paul. An important work.   248.6.W69

Church Management

Armerding, Hudson T. *Leadership.* Wheaton, IL: Tyndale House Publishers, 1978.

Based squarely on the Scriptures, these chapters discuss thirteen aspects of Christian leadership that must be mastered and applied if success in any area of service is to be assured.   262.1.AR5

*Baughen, Michael. *The Moses Principle: Leadership and the Venture of Faith.* Wheaton, IL: Harold Shaw Publishers, 1979.

Discusses the spiritual and administrative skills which made Moses a man of God and the emancipator of the people of Israel.

248.4.B32

Cosgrove, Francis M., Jr. *Essentials of Discipleship.* Colorado Springs, CO: Navpress, 1980.

In clear, unmistakable terms, Cosgrove cuts across traditional ecclesiastical mores and charts a course for the development of disciples that is at once biblical and practical. Recommended.   248.27.C82

Deweese, Charles W. *The Emerging Role of Deacons.* Nashville: Broadman Press, 1979.

Explains the effect of changing times on the role and function of the deacon in Southern Baptist Churches.   262.1.D51

Drucker, Peter Ferdinand. *Managing in Turbulent Times.* New York: Harper and Row, 1980.

Important and timely, these chapters concentrate the reader's attention on trends in business, society, and the economy. Issues like inflation, population, and production are documented and discussed with the author's usual foresight and vigor. Preachers will find this volume both stimulating and enlightening. Recommended.   658.D84T

Fordyce, Jack K., and **Raymond Weil.** *Managing With People: A Manager's Handbook of Organizational Development Methods.* 2d. ed. Reading, MA: Addison-Wesley Publishing Company, 1979.

Pastors who would like to learn how to accomplish more through others will welcome this handy, well-outlined, thoroughly-researched little volume. It is replete with ideas, procedures, and counsel. Secular.

658.4.F75 1979

Hunt, James G., and **Lars L. Larson,** eds. *Crosscurrents in Leadership.* Carbondale, IL: Southern Illinois University Press, 1979.

Contains papers read at the 1978 Leadership Symposia, Southern Illinois University. An excellent resource which, together with the other volumes in this series, should be of particular interest to D.Min. students.

xxxxxxxxxxxxxxxxxxxxxxxxxxxxxxxxxxxx 301.15.C88 1979

Parkinson, Cyril Northcote. *Parkinson: The Law.* Boston: Houghton Mifflin Company, 1980.

"Parkinson's Law" is as famous as "The Peter Principle." And here, for the benefit of those who no longer have access to the 1957 edition, is a revised and updated version with several new "laws." Excellent as satire; devastating in its critique of bureaucrats and their methods.   350.P22 1980

*Richards, Lawrence O., and Clyde Hoeldtke. *A Theology of Church Leadership.* Grand Rapids: Zondervan Publishing House, 1980.
Seminal in nature, this assessment of the needs of the church denounces authoritarian and secular methods of managerial leadership, and stresses instead the authority of the Word, submission to Christ as the true Head, and a style of servant leadership which is dynamically different from the usual methodologies practiced by many "shepherds" today.   262.1.R39T

Schaller, Lyle E. *The Multiple Staff and the Larger Church.* Nashville: Abingdon Press, 1980.
Written for larger churches, this book dis-cusses the many alternatives of staffing churches. Includes the place and use of volunteers as well as the duties that can be carried on by others.   253.SCH1M

Smith, Barth. *A Pastor's Handbook of Church Management.* Kansas City, MO: Beacon Hill Press, 1978.
Following a traditional outline (planning, organizing, leading, controlling), Smith handles the usual subdivisions skillfully and with specific application to the pastoral ministry.   254.SM5

*Smith, Harold T., and William H. Baker. *The Administrative Manager.* Chicago: Science Research Associates, 1978.
D.Min. students in church administration and pastors lacking training in management will find this volume to be "made-to-order." It covers the principle areas of administration, shows how effective leaders operate, and provides extensive sections on motivation, communication, personnel management, etc. Excellent.   651.SM5

Pastoral Counseling

Adams, Jay Edward. *More Than Redemption: A Theology of Christian Counseling.* Grand Rapids: Baker Book House, 1979.
From this prolific author comes a work relating the different areas of theology to counseling. Informative, but gives the impression of being forced or contrived. Areas of practical usefulness include habits, prayer, suffering, new converts, good works, etc.   253.5.AD1M

Bailey, Robert W. *Ministering to the Grieving.* Grand Rapids: Zondervan Publishing House, 1980.
A handy manual for pastor and counselor. Follows the reality-oriented model of therapy.   253.5.B15

Brown, Raymond Kay. *Reach Out to Singles: A Challenge to Ministry.* Philadelphia: Westminster Press, 1979.
Examines the hard questions single people are asking, and attempts to provide candid and helpful answers. An important work for pastors.   261.8'34.B81

*Carkhuff. Robert R., with R. M. Pierce and J. R. Cannon. *The Art of Helping, IV.* Amherst, MA: Human Resource Development Press, 1980.
Most informative and practical. Ideal for all who are in the helping professions.   253.5.C19

Carter, John Daniel, and Stanley Bruce Narramore. *The Integration of Psychology and Theology: An Introduction.* Grand Rapids: Zondervan Publishing House, 1979.
The first in the Rosemead Psychology Series, this work consists of articles which initially appeared in the *Journal of Psychology and Theology.*   261.5.C24

Clements, William M. *Care and Counseling of the Aging.* Philadelphia: Fortress Press, 1979.
Focuses on geriatrics and the personal problems of the aging. Seeks to integrate the problems faced by senior citizens with the down-to-earth realities of ministry to older people.   253.5.C59

———. *Ministry With the Aging.* San Francisco: Harper and Row, 1981.
Building upon the solid research of gerontologists, psychologists, historians, and theo-

logians, Clements applies the truths gleaned to the problems of the aged and the way in which the church can meet their needs.

259'.3.C59

Clinebell, Howard John. *Contemporary Growth Therapies: Resources for Actualizing Human Wholeness.* Nashville: Abingdon Press, 1980.

This companion volume to *Growth Counseling: Hope-Centered Methods of Actualizing Human Wholeness* (1979) is a departure from Freudian psychoanalysis and concentrates on different models of therapy with a view to helping the counselor develop skills that will facilitate the growth of the counselee. Recommended.

616.89'14.C61C

———. *Growth Counseling: Hope-Centered Methods of Actualizing Wholeness.* Nashville: Abingdon Press, 1979.

A further elaboration of the author's growth counseling model of therapy. Achieves success through focusing on the potentials of individuals rather than discussing their emotions or advocating change through behavioral modification. In this book Clinebell describes the principles, methods, and theological presuppositions of his system.

253.5.C61G 1979

Coleman, William L. *Understanding Suicide.* Elgin, IL: David C. Cook Publishing Company, 1979.

Treats suicide from the point of view of the potential victim. Lays bare the causes and shows pastors how to handle this kind of situation should one arise in the church. Recommended.

362.2.C67

Collins, Gary R. *Christian Counseling: A Comprehensive Guide.* Waco, TX: Word Books, 1980.

Nearly five hundred pages in length, this is Collins' most exhaustive work to date. In brief format, the author treats all of the major areas of personality without enlarging upon neurotic and psychotic disorders.

253.5.C69C 1980

Coote, Robert T., and **John R. W. Stott**, eds. *Down to Earth: Studies in Christianity and Culture.* Grand Rapids: Wm. B. Eerdmans Publishing Co., 1980.

These papers, delivered at the "Lausanne Consultation on Gospel and Culture" contain some excellent chapters by well-known authors, but most of them are deficient in biblical content. Disappointing.

262'.001.D75 1980

Cosgrove, Mark P. *Psychology Gone Awry: Analysis of Psychological World Views.* Grand Rapids: Zondervan Publishing House, 1979.

A sorely needed treatise which examines the presuppositions of naturalistic, humanistic, and transpersonal psychologies and finds them wanting; and in their place suggests a distinctively different approach based on the *imago Dei.*

150'.1.C82P

Fairchild, Roy W. *Finding Hope Again: A Pastor's Guide to Counseling Depressed Persons.* San Francisco: Harper and Row, 1980.

Focuses on the causes of depression and advises pastors how to counsel depressed persons. Excellent.

253.5.F16

Feigenberg, Loma. *Terminal Care: Friendship Contacts with Dying Cancer Patients.* Translated by P. Hort. New York: Brunner/Mazel, 1980.

After a lifetime of work in the area of thanatology, the author shares her insights into the most productive way to work with terminally ill patients. Compassionate, humane. Truly helpful.

616'029.F32

Fretz, Bruce R., and **David H. Mills.** *Licensing and Certification of Psychologists and Counselors: A Guide to Current Policies, Procedures, and Legislation.* San Francisco: Jossey-Bass Publishers, 1980.

Ably fulfills the subtitle. Provides essential insights for those engaged in structuring ministerial counseling programs.

351.82.F89

Hamilton, Michael Pollock, and **Helen F. Reid.** *A Hospice Handbook: A New Way to Care for the Dying.* Grand Rapids: Wm. B. Eerdmans Publishing Company, 1980.

Each chapter in this book was contributed by a specialist. It surveys the distinctive needs of patients and discusses such areas as relief from pain and fear, and the skills required by doctors and nurses.

362.1.H79

Hauck, Paul A. *Brief Counseling with RET.* Philadelphia: Westminster Press, 1980.

Describes the fundamentals of effective, short-term counseling using RET—Rational Emotive Therapy. Included is a description of how various problems and personality disorders may be treated. Pastors will find the discussion highly informative.

616.89.H29B 1980

Headington, Bonnie Joy. *Communication in the Counseling Relationship.* Cranston, RI: Carroll Press, 1979.

Combining theory with practice, Headington comes to grips with this fundamental issue of counseling, *viz.*, communication, and explains the principles with sensitivity and skill. Recommended. 253.5.H34

Hiltner, Seward. *Theological Dynamics.* Nashville: Abingdon Press, 1980.
†One of the pioneer works in the correlation of psychology and theology. Insightful.
261.5.H56 1980

Hoffman, John Charles. *Ethical Confrontation in Counseling.* Chicago: University of Chicago Press, 1979.
Appeals for a "more consistent and enthusiastic moral witness at the very heart of the psychotherapeutic process. . . ." Secular.
253.5.H67

Hulme, William Edward. *How to Start Counseling.* Nashville: Abingdon Press, 1979.
Originally published in 1955, this introductory work is ideally suited to the needs of the pastor who has not had formal training in counseling. Recommended. 253.5.H87 1979

Jacobson, Neil S., and **Gayla Margolin.** *Marital Therapy: Strategies Based on Social Learning and Behavior Exchange Principles.* New York: Brunner/Mazel, 1979.
The authors show how "behavior exchange principles" can be employed to alter communication patterns and "no-win" situations, and assist in the solving of marital problems. Of interest to pastors as well as counselors.
253.5.J15 (Alt. DDC 362.8'2)

Kerr, Horace L. *How to Minister to Senior Adults in Your Church.* Nashville: Broadman Press, 1980.
One of the most comprehensive manuals on this facet of the church's ministry. A vital book. 259.K46

Kopp, Ruth Lewshenia, with **Stephen Sorenson.** *Encounter with Terminal Illness.* Grand Rapids: Zondervan Publishing House, 1980.
Counsel from a physician on how the patient and his family may be prepared for death. A *must* for pastoral counselors. 248.86.K83

Koteskey, Ronald L. *Psychology from a Christian Perspective.* Nashville: Abingdon Press, 1980.
Discusses the role of psychology in the world today, warns against its abuse, explains the rise of different psychological systems, and then handles different issues within the discipline from an integrative point of view.
150.19.K84

Kutash, Irwin L.; **Louis B. Schlesinger**; and Associates. *Handbook on Stress and Anxiety.* San Francisco: Jossey-Bass Publishers, 1980.
Treats the dramatic upward spiral of stress and anxiety cases in commerce and industry, and describes how counselors may play a part in reducing these destructive tendencies.
152.4.K96

Leslie, Robert C. *Sharing Groups in the Church: An Invitation to Involvement.* Nashville: Abingdon Press, 1979.
First published a decade ago, this practical work introduces pastors and counselors to the needs of people in the church and the way in which these needs may be met through small care groups. 254.6.L56

Lieberman, Morton A., et al. *Self-Help Groups for Coping with Crisis.* San Francisco: Jossey-Bass Publishers, 1979.
Of interest to pastors, for it focuses on two types of care groups—those designed to modify their members' behavior or attitudes (including groups for alcoholics and their families, for child abusers, or for former mental patients) and those formed to aid in coping with particular life crises (ranging from a major illness to aging to the loss of one's spouse or child)—groups which can and should function as a part of the *koinonia* of the local church. 361.7.L62

Linn, Dennis, and **Matthew Linn.** *Healing Life's Hurts: Healing Memories Through Five Stages of Forgiveness.* New York: Paulist Press, 1978.
One of the finest works ever written on the subject of forgiveness. Includes a section on sacramentalism. Roman Catholic.
248.4.L64

Linn, Mary Jane; **Matthew Linn**; and **Dennis Linn.** *Healing the Dying: Releasing People to Die.* New York: Paulist Press, 1979.
Using the seven final acts and words of Christ on the cross, these dedicated Roman Catholics treat the care that can be extended to the dying and their families. 242.4.L64

Matheny, Kenneth B., and **Richard J. Riordan.** *Therapy American Style: Person Power Through Self-Help.* Chicago: Nelson-Hall, 1979.
More than just another "self-help" book, this work lays a foundation for personal change through a practical approach to therapy and actualization that paves the way for growth, the reduction of stress, and the opening of the channels of communication.
158.1.M42

Norman, William H., and **Thomas J. Scaramella**. *Mid-Life Developmental and Clinical Issues*. New York: Brunner/Mazel, 1980.

This symposium draws attention to nine separate facets of mid-life crisis. Explains the strains and challenges, and helps those in this period of life understand what is happening, why, and what they can do about it. Helpful.
616.89.M58

Ogden, Schubert Miles. *Faith and Freedom: Toward a Theology of Liberation*. Nashville: Abingdon Press, 1979.

†Traces the background and development of modern liberation theologies, analyzes their strengths and weaknesses, and points out their failures. Lacks unction.
261.8.0G2

Perez, Joseph Francis. *Family Counseling: Theory and Practice*. New York: D. Van Nostrand Company, 1979.

Combining both an historic introduction to family counseling and a treatment of theoretical issues and techniques, this work could be used in seminary counseling programs.
616.8915.P41

Puryear, Douglas A. *Helping People in Crisis*. San Francisco: Jossey-Bass Publishers, 1979.

Of value to paraprofessionals in the ministry of counseling. Treats the interview step by step, from first contact to cessation of therapy. Valuable for its insights.
616.8'915.P97

Schmidt, Paul F. *Coping with Difficult People*. Philadelphia: Westminster Press, 1980.

A brief introduction to different types of personality disorders. Ideal for those in the church with little or no previous training in personality theory.
616.85.SCH5

Seligman, Linda. *Assessment in Developmental Career Counseling*. Cranston, RI: Carroll Press, 1980.

A helpful book for the pastoral counselor who works with young people.
650.1'4.S4

Stahmann, Robert F., and **William J. Hiebert.** *Premarital Counseling*. Lexington, MA: Lexington Books, 1980.

Written by two members of the American Association of Marriage and Family Therapy, this slender but helpful volume covers the foundations of marriage, conjoint counseling of engaged couples, group premarital counseling, and topics of special interest to counselors. An excellent introduction.
253.5.ST1

Stewart, Charles William. *The Minister as Family Counselor*. Nashville: Abingdon Press, 1979.

Designed for pastors. Through the use of charts and diagrams, the author describes the family structure, pinpoints the causes of family breakdown, and shows what pastors may do to prevent predicaments from arising.
253.5.ST4

Homiletics

Achtemeier, Elizabeth. *Creative Preaching: Finding the Words*. Nashville: Abingdon Press, 1980.

Of value to novice and veteran alike, this handbook on the art of homiletics stresses the importance of language. Topics discussed are style, logic, the mental images created, the principles of effective communication, and motivation. Underscores the importance of creativity and stresses the place of the Bible in the ministry of the Word.
251.AC4

Daane, James. *Preaching with Confidence: A Theological Essay on the Power of the Pulpit*. Grand Rapids: Wm. B. Eerdmans Publishing Co., 1980.

Believing that, when God's Word is preached with confidence, people change, Daane sets out to describe the fundamental task of every preacher to proclaim the Word of the Lord.
251.D11

Demaray, Donald E. *Proclaiming the Truth: Guides to Scriptural Preaching*. Grand Rapids: Baker Book House, 1979.

Contains material not found in other works. Covers the areas of orientation, preparation, and communication. Includes an appendix on "One Hundred Books for the Preacher's Library."
251'.01.D39

Dodd, Charles Harold. *The Apostolic Preaching and Its Developments, With an Appendix on Eschatology and History*. Grand Rapids: Baker Book House, 1980.

An epochal series of lectures which, when first delivered at King's College, London, in 1935, started a new trend in homiletics. Stimulating.
251'.008.D66

Fisher, Wallace E. *Who Dares to Preach? The Challenge of Biblical Preaching*. Minneapolis: Augsburg Publishing House, 1979.

A veteran in the art and science of homiletics reveals the basic principles and philosophy which has molded his own approach to the ministry of the pulpit.   251'.01.F53

Ford, D. W. Cleverley. *The Ministry of the Word.* Grand Rapids: Wm. B. Eerdmans Publishing Co., 1979.
Treats the sermons of the Bible, the opportunities and responsibilities of modern preachers of the Word, and the methodology for preparing a biblical sermon with insight and skill. Recommended.   251.F75M

Forsyth, Peter Taylor. *Positive Preaching and the Modern Mind.* Grand Rapids: Baker Book House, 1980.
Comprising the Lyman Beecher Lectures on Preaching, Yale University, 1907, this volume contains Forsyth's explication of the minister's charge and authority, and the manner and means of effective communication.
251.F77

Fuller, Reginald Horace. *The Use of the Bible in Preaching.* Philadelphia: Fortress Press, 1981.
Working within the framework of theological liberalism, Fuller attempts to show that the Bible has not lost its authority, but that its message still can be made relevant to the needs of modern man.   251.F95

Johnson, Samuel. *Sermons.* Ed. by J. Hagstrom and J. Gray. New Haven, CT: Yale University Press, 1978.
The first scholarly edition of Johnson's sermons. Will please students of homiletics.
252.J63

Kroll, Woodrow Michael. *Prescription for Preaching.* Grand Rapids: Baker Book House, 1980.
Differing from other works on homiletics, this treatment of the theory and practice of public speaking aims at excellence in delivery as a result of thorough, intelligent, meaningful preparation. Worthy of careful consideration.   251.03.K85

Perry, Lloyd Merle, and **John R. Strubbar.** *Evangelistic Preaching.* Chicago: Moody Press, 1979.
A clear presentation of the difference between homiletic sermonizing and true evangelistic preaching. Surveys trends in evangelism from the earliest times to the present.   253.P42E

Prochnow, Herbert V., and **Herbert V. Prochnow, Jr.** *The Toastmaster's Treasure Chest.* New York: Harper and Row, 1979.
A valuable resource for pastors to either spice up sermons, introduce a visiting speaker, or enliven a conversation.   080'.24.P94 1979

***Robinson, Haddon W.** *Biblical Preaching: The Development and Delivery of Expository Messages.* Grand Rapids: Baker Book House, 1980.
Drawing upon his extensive experience as a preacher and homiletics professor, Robinson describes the way in which preachers may make their messages clear, direct, vivid, and convincing. An excellent work—possibly the best work on the subject.   251.3.R56

Tan, Paul Lee. *Encyclopedia of 7,700 Illustrations.* Rockville, MD: Assurance Publishers, 1979.
As a general rule books of illustrations are seldom worth purchasing. This work is an exception. "Of all the books of illustrations currently available, this *Encyclopedia* stands quite alone. Despite the reservations one must always have regarding such works, this one can be confidently recommended."—*Bibliotheca Sacra.*   251'.08.T15

***Wiersbe, Warren W.** *Listening to the Giants: A Guide to Good Reading and Great Preaching.* Grand Rapids: Baker Book House, 1980.
A delightful book adequately sketching the life and contribution of some of the world's greatest preachers, and then supplying one of their sermons. Includes an important chapter on "A Basic Library" for every pastor.
251'.009.W63

Willimon, William H., and **Robert Leroy Wilson.** *Preaching and Worship in the Small Church.* Nashville: Abingdon Press, 1980.
Shows how "small" can be beautiful, and how a small church can have a dynamic fellowship. Lamentably focuses on externals as opposed to fellowship. Nonetheless, insightful.
253.W67

Chapter 9

MISSIONS

Bosch, David J. *Witness to the World: The Christian Mission in Theological Perspective.* Atlanta: John Knox Press, 1980.

Published simultaneously in the U.S. and U.K., this insightful study contributes immeasurably toward an understanding of missionary impact around the world, particularly as shaped by political and theological opinion—both from the left wing and the right—and modified by Third World churches. 262'.001.B65

Cowan, George M. *The Word That Kindles.* Chappaqua, NY: Christian Herald Books, 1979.

More than just another book on modern missions, this work emphasizes the dedication and skills which are required of Wycliffe Bible translators. It is also replete with encouraging accounts of those who have preceded contemporary translators in the ministry. 266'.023.C83W

Falk, Peter. *The Growth of the Church in Africa.* Grand Rapids: Zondervan Publishing House, 1979.

A careful history by a pastor and missionary to Zaire. Includes a discussion of conditions affecting the spread of Christianity, a survey of missionary methods, and a consideration of the Africa Independent Church movement. 276.F18

Grunlan, Stephen A., and **Marvin K. Mayers.** *Cultural Anthropology: A Christian Perspective.* Grand Rapids: Zondervan Publishing House, 1979.

Directed to Bible school students, this sociological treatise seeks to explain the basis of cultural diversities in an endeavor to help evangelical students minister cross-culturally. Recommended. 301.2.G92

Hesselgrave, David J., ed. *New Horizons in World Mission.* Grand Rapids: Baker Book House, 1979.

Contains messages delivered at the Second Consultation on Theology and Mission, Trinity Evangelical Divinity School, IL, 1979. Lays a solid foundation for missions in the 80s. 266'.008.H46 1979

Hick, John, and **Brian Habblewaite.** *Christianity and Other Religions.* Philadelphia: Fortress Press, 1980.

Excerpts material from the writings of men such as Ernst Troeltsch, Karl Barth, Karl Rahner, Paul Tillich, etc., to demonstrate the wide range of attitudes toward other faiths. Does so with the intention of providing a basis for inter-faith dialog while affirming the uniqueness of Christianity. 261.2.C46

Kane, J. Herbert. *Life and Work on the Mission Field.* Grand Rapids: Baker Book House, 1980.

Charts a course through the shoals of missionary work and gives to prospective missionaries numerous valuable ideas based on the author's many years of service abroad. Treats adequately aspects of missionary preparation, life on the field, and the work to be done. 266.K13L 1980

Kirk, J. Andrew. *Liberation Theology: An Evangelical View of the Third World.* Atlanta: John Knox Press, 1979.

Surveys the roots of liberation theology and assesses the contribution of five of the most influential "liberation" thinkers. Looks at the application of this form of theology to the Latin American scene, and concludes with a view of the way these theologians approach the Scriptures and the fundamentals of the faith. 262.8.K63

McGavran, Donald Anderson. *Understanding Church Growth.* Grand Rapids: Wm. B. Eerdmans Publishing Co., 1980.

Fully revised after ten years in circulation, and with three new chapters added, this foundational treatise will continue to be one of *the* most important works on church growth.

266.M17U 1980

Ramsden, William E. *The Church in a Changing Society.* Nashville: Abingdon Press, 1980.

Another work sponsored by the United Methodist Church, assessing change within society and charting a course for the church in the future. Serves as a model for other organizations.   287.673.R14

Steven, Hugh. *Never Touch a Tiger.* Nashville: Thomas Nelson Publishers, 1980.

While reading like a novel, this account of missionary work in Central and South America by Wycliffe Bible translators conveys some of the humor and challenge of missions.

266'.023.J63.ST4

Chapter 10

CHRISTIAN EDUCATION

Allen, Charles Livingstone, and **Mildred Parker.** *How to Increase Your Sunday School Attendance.* Old Tappan, NJ: Fleming H. Revell Company, 1979.

Two veterans in the field of Christian education team up and show how a vigorous Sunday school ministry can build a church.
268.AL3

Bossant, Donald E. *Creative Conflict in Religious Education and Church Administration.* Birmingham, AL: Religious Education Press, 1980.

Describes conflict—theological, psychological, and sociological—and shows how an understanding of its dynamics may assist educators and administrators to turn conflict into an asset that will work for them instead of a liability which works against them.
254.B65

Boys, Mary C. *Biblical Interpretation in Religious Education: A Study of the Kerygmatic Era.* Birmingham, AL: Religious Education Press, 1980.

Written with Roman Catholics in mind, this informative and perceptive recounting of the history of biblical interpretation and its impact on parochial education stresses the role of *Heilsgeschichte* and the importance of ecumenical dialogue if meaningful progress is to be made. Needs to be read with discernment.
220.6.B71

Cochrane, Donald B.; **Cornel M. Hamm**; and **Anastasios C. Kazepides**, eds. *The Domain of Moral Education.* New York: Paulist Press, 1979.

This symposium introduces the reader to various ways in which people have tended to think erroneously about moral problems and thus escape the demands of moral thinking. Following this, the contributors explore the heart of moral education with a view to providing moral principles for conduct as well as education.
370'.114.D71

Groome, Thomas H. *Christian Religious Education: Sharing Our Story and Vision.* San Francisco: Harper and Row, 1980.

Giving evidence of real sophistication, yet readable and nonparochial, this work makes a unique contribution to the nature, purpose, context, and approach of religious education.
268'.01.G89

Lockerbie, D. Bruce. *Who Educates Your Child? A Book for Parents.* Garden City, NY: Doubleday and Company, 1980.

Fully cognizant of the current dilemma facing Christian parents, Lockerbie cuts through the intellectual, political, and emotional confusion. By placing the responsibility squarely where it belongs, he provides wise counsel for parents . . . as well as educators. Recommended.
370.1.L79W

Lynn, Robert W., and **H. Elliott Wright.** *The Big Little School: Two Hundred Years of the Sunday School.* 2d ed. Revised. Birmingham, AL: Religious Education Press, 1980.

Commemorates the two hundred years of the Sunday school in the U.S. Analyzes the reasons for its success and explains the origins of the problems presently being experienced in Sunday schools across the country.
268'.09.L99

Miller, Randolph Crump. *The Theory of Christian Education Practice: How Theology Affects Christian Education.* Birmingham, AL: Religious Education Press, 1980.

A lucid application of theological truths to educational principles. Ably blends theory and practice. Recommended for a serious discussion. Will be appreciated by CE majors.
207.M61

Murray, Lawrence L. *The Celluloid Persuasion: Movies and the Liberal Arts.* Grand Rapids: Wm. B. Eerdmans Publishing Co., 1979.

Described as a "nuts-and-bolts" approach to the use of film materials, this work shows how the use of audio-visual equipment can enhance classroom education. A *must* for DCEs.   378.1'7.M96

Willis, Wesley R. *Two Hundred Years—and Still Counting.* Wheaton, IL: Victor Books, 1979.

An intriguing story of the history and accomplishments of the Sunday school, together with an assessment of what remains to be done.   268'.009.W67

Zaccaria, Joseph S., and **Stephen G. Bopp.** *Approaches to Guidance in Contemporary Education.* 2d ed. Cranston, RI: Carroll Press, 1980.

Surveys guidance counseling within the context of the school and explores guidance counseling within the context of our contemporary society. Compares policies in the U.S. with the practices of educational institutions in other countries. Of value to the pastor who, of necessity, must frequently counsel young people in the church regarding their career choice.   371.4.Z1 1980

Chapter 11

CHURCH HISTORY AND BIOGRAPHY

Historiography

Bainton, Roland Herbert. *Yesterday, Today, and What Next? Reflections on History and Hope*. Minneapolis: Augsburg Publishing House, 1978.
Important reflections on history and its lessons for us today.   901.B16

Bebbington, David W. *Patterns in History:* *A Christian View*. Downers Grove, IL: InterVarsity Press, 1979.
Develops a philosophy of historiography, but omits the Kingdom concept which is so much a part of biblical revelation in both testaments. The author's critiques of the cyclical theory, the idea of progress, historicism, Marxism, etc., are of great value.   901.B38

History of the Church

Butterfield, Herbert. *Writings on Christianity and History*. Edited by C. T. McIntire. New York: Oxford University Press, 1979.
By limiting himself to data which can be verified by scientific historiography, the author of this collection of essays (written over a period of nearly thirty years) deals with the major movements of Christianity and the people behind them.   230.'09.B98

Church, F. F., and T. George. *Continuity and Discontinuity in Church History: Essays Presented to George Hunston William*. Leiden, The Netherlands: E. J. Brill, 1979.
Contains 26 essays by leading church historians. Reflects (1) "Communion and Atonement," (2) "The Radical Reformation," and (3) "Wilderness and Paradise" in the experiences of different religious movements. Stimulating.   270'.08.C74

Eck, John. *Enchiridion of Commonplaces Against Luther and Other Enemies of the Church*. Translated by Ford Lewis Battles. Grand Rapids: Baker Book House, 1979.
First published in 1529, this work provides a background for the Reformation debates and the controversies of that period. As such, it is a valuable resource. Roman Catholic.
270.6.EC5 1979

Edwards, David L. *Christian England: Its Story to the Reformation*. New York: Oxford University Press, 1980.
Written from the perspective of Roman Catholicism, this work discusses in broad outline the events which now provide the religious heritage of the English-speaking people.   274.42.ED9

Ellul, Jacques. *The Betrayal of the West*. Translated by M. J. O'Connell. New York: Seabury Press, 1978.
This candid assessment of occidental civilization indicts those of a theologically "liberal" persuasion for undermining the very culture which gave them the benefits of freedom and the blessings of democracy which they now enjoy. The need, which Ellul fails to recognize, is for a return to the principles of the Reformation (or, more specifically, to the authority of Scripture), which paved the way for the development of our Western culture.   909'.09'821.EL5B

Hengel, Martin. *Jews, Greeks and Barbarians: Aspects of the Hellenization of Judaism in the pre-Christian Period*. Translated by J. Bowden. Philadelphia: Fortress Press, 1980.
Deals with the political and social history

of Palestine from the time of Alexander the Great to Antiochus Epiphanes. Discusses the spread of Hellenism and the experience of the Jews of the Diaspora.   930.H38

Hiscox, Edward T. *Principles and Practices of Baptist Churches.* Grand Rapids: Kregel Publications, 1980.
First published in 1894 under the title *New Directory for Baptist Churches*, this book is designed to provide clearly defined guidelines for the functioning of Baptist churches while preserving the autonomy of each local assembly.   286.H62 1980

Hort, Fenton John Anthony. *Judiastic Christianity.* Edited by J. O. F. Murray. Grand Rapids: Baker Book House, 1980.
First published in 1894, these studies of the history of the Apostolic and Post-Apostolic Periods reveal the basic incompatibility of Christianity and Judaism. Valuable for collateral reading in courses on ecclesiology.   296.3.H78 1980

McKinley, Edward H. *Marching to Glory: The History of the Salvation Army in the United States of America, 1880-1980.* San Francisco: Harper and Row, 1980.
From its insignificant beginnings a century ago, McKinley traces the rise of the Salvation Army, their "dough-nut" ministries, involvement in prohibition, work during the Depression, and social welfare work.   267.15.M21

Neal, Daniel. *The History of the Puritans;* . . . 3 vols. Minneapolis: Klock and Klock Christian Publishers, 1979.
Reprinted from the latest edition and containing critical notes, this outstanding presentation of Protestant nonconformity from 1517 to 1688 delineates the course of action taken by those dubbed "Puritan," describes the seeds of liberty and democracy which they spread and which lie inherent in their history and teachings, and presents a vivid picture of

the effect of their stand for the truth. Worthy of serious study.   285.9.N25 1979

Rifkin, Jeremy, with **Ted Howard.** *The Emerging Order: God in the Age of Scarcity.* New York: G. P. Putnam's Sons, 1979.
Whereas Toffler's *Future Shock* had the effect of providing excuses for further lowering of moral standards, this book indicts the liberal trend toward socialism and stresses the areas of cultural importance in which evangelical Christianity can play a vital role. Provocative.   277.3.R44

Toon, Peter. *Evangelical Theology, 1833-1856: A Response to Tractarianism.* Atlanta: John Knox Press, 1979.
A brilliant study of the Oxford Movement and the influence of Newman, Pusey, and Keble on early Tractarianism.   283.41.T6

Wells, William W. *Welcome to the Family: An Introduction to Evangelical Christianity.* Downers Grove, IL: InterVarsity Press, 1979.
Beginning with the Bible, its origin, and principles of interpretation, Wells shows how in NT times believers became part of a new community and were thus able to withstand adversity. In the history of the church, whenever persecution broke out, the same sense of belonging sustained them. Wells continues to trace this familial theme through the Reformation to the present. He uses this sense of community to strengthen believers to reach out to others.   280.4.W46

Workman, Herbert B. *Persecution in the Early Church.* New York: Oxford University Press, 1980.
This important assessment of persecution in the early centuries of the Christian era analyzes the clash between church and state, probes the causes of hatred, chronicles the great persecutions, and recounts the experiences of the persecuted.   272.1.W89

Biography

Ayling, Stanley. *John Wesley.* Nashville: Abingdon Press, 1979.
A full-length portrait of the "father of Methodism" by an authority on eighteenth-century church history. Stimulating.   287.W51.AY4

Bruce, Frederick Fyvie. *In Retrospect: Remembrance of Things Past.* Grand Rapids: Wm. B. Eerdmans Publishing Co., 1980.

Brief chapters, partly historical and partly topical, in which Bruce recalls significant events throughout his long, scholarly life. Includes discourses on his friends, a discussion on his love of books, and a description of his literary activities.   286.542.B83

Clark, Clifford E. *Henry Ward Beecher, Spokesman for a Middle-class America.* Urbana, IL: University of Illinois Press, 1978.

Based on extensive research into primary sources, Clark examines Beecher's many roles and his impact as a liberal on the major reform movements of his era. 285'.8.B39.C54

*Dallimore, Arnold A. *George Whitefield: The Life and Times of the Great Evangelist of the Eighteenth-Century Revival*. Vol. 2. Westchester, IL: Cornerstone Books, 1979.
At last, after several years of delay, the author has provided us with the concluding volume. He picks up from where he left off in Vol. 1 and provides us with insights into Whitefield's relationship with the Wesleys, discusses the controversies which plagued his later years, describes his evangelistic work on two continents, etc. All things considered, this is a very human work. It concludes with an extensive bibliography. Recommended. 285.873.W58D v.2

Doig, Desmond. *Mother Teresa: Her People and Her Work*. San Francisco: Harper and Row, 1980.
First published in 1976, this touching book chronicles in pictures as well as words the life, labors, and accomplishments of Mother Teresa, a remarkable humanitarian and deserved winner of the Nobel Peace Prize. 266.2.T27.D68

Drewery, Mary. *William Carey: A Biography*. Grand Rapids: Zondervan Publishing House, 1979.
Discusses the crises, both spiritual and personal, of Carey's life and provides a captivating account of his missionary vision and venture of faith. 266.6.C18.D82

Dunker, Marilee Pierce. *Man of Vision; Woman of Prayer*. Nashville: Thomas Nelson Publishers, 1980.
A candid inside look at the lives of the author's parents, their ministry to the underprivileged around the world, and the pain of separation. 269.2.P61.D92

Ericson, Edward E., Jr. *Solzhenitsyn: The Moral Vision*. Grand Rapids: Wm. B. Eerdmans Publishing Co., 1980.
Written before the publication of *The Oak and the Calf*, this work traces Aleksandr Solzhenitsyn's life through his writings. Valuable for its interpretative approach. 891.73'44.ER4

Hardesty, Nancy A. *Great Women of Faith: The Strength and Influence of Christian Women*. Grand Rapids: Baker Book House, 1980.

No one will dispute the old adage that "the hand that rocks the cradle rules the world." In these brief, informative chapters readers are not only reminded of this fact but are given the impression that *Great Women of the Faith* is being used as a vehicle for propaganda. Disappointing. 922.H21

Hopkins, C. Howard. *John R. Mott, 1865-1955: A Biography*. Grand Rapids: Wm. B. Eerdmans Publishing Co., 1979.
Stressing the ecumenical influence of Mott, his biographer also describes how the provincial Midwestern youth became one of the most influential men of his generation. Includes accounts of Mott's struggles, failures, and successes. Inspirational reading. 267'.392.M85.H77

Hunter, Ian. *Malcolm Muggeridge: A Life*. Nashville: Thomas Nelson Publishers, 1980.
Chronicles the fascinating saga of Muggeridge's varied and full life. Describes his conversion from agnosticism to Christianity, and the events that followed. Well researched. 070.92'4.M89.H92

Olivier, Daniel A. A. *The Trial of Luther*. Translated by J. Tonkin. St. Louis: Concordia Publishing House, 1979.
First published in 1971, and making use of original sources, this work deals concisely with the events surrounding Luther's trial, 1517–1521. 270.6.L97.0L4 1979

Sainsbury, R. M. *Russell*. London: Routledge and Kegan Paul, 1979.
Describes the growth of Bertrand Russell's ideas, but fails to account for or defend his rejection of Christianity. Of value to those interested in philosophy. 192.R91.S2

Smith, Warren Thomas. *Augustine: His Life and Thought*. Atlanta: John Knox Press, 1980.
Ably combines biographical facts relating to Augustine's life with the history of the times and the development of his beliefs. Scholarly, readable, stimulating. 281.4.AU4.S6

Snyder, Howard A. *The Radical Wesley and Patterns for Church Renewal*. Downers Grove, IL: InterVarsity Press, 1980.
Writing out of a heart of concern for the church, Snyder uses Wesley as a model of spiritual-sociological renewal. He then applies principles from Wesley's work to the task facing Christians today. Missing, however, is a biblical foundation. Absent, too, is a discussion of the weaknesses attending any human movement. 287.W51.S9

Wesley, Charles. *The Journal of Charles Wesley.* 2 Vols. Grand Rapids: Baker Book House, 1980.

Photographically reproduced from the 1849 edition, this reprint makes available to modern readers the journal, poetry, and correspondence of this great leader of the Christian church.   287.142.W51 1980

White, William, Jr. *Van Til: Defender of the Faith.* Nashville: Thomas Nelson Publishers, 1979.

Views the theology and apologetics of Cornelius Van Til in the context of his times. Provides interesting and informative sidelights on his contemporaries. A worthy acquisition.

285.731.V36.W58

Chapter 12

COMPARATIVE RELIGIONS AND CULTS

Anderson, Robert Maples. *Vision of the Disinherited: The Making of American Pentecostalism.* New York: Oxford University Press, 1979.
A study of the formative phrase of the Pentecostal movement from the latter part of the nineteenth century to the early 1930s. Treats the three major divisions of Pentecostalism. 289.9.AN2

Arrington, Leonard J., and **Davis Bitton.** *The Mormon Experience: A History of the Latter-day Saints.* New York: Alfred A. Knopf, 1979.
A pro-Mormon history of the origin and growth of the movement containing information from Mormon archives previously not available to researchers. 289.3'09.AR6

Baxter, James Sidlon. *Divine Healing of the Body.* Grand Rapids: Zondervan Publishing House, 1979.
Considers the evidence for divine healing through the centuries and then takes a sober look at divine healing as it is taught today. 289.9.B33

Boyce, Mary. *Zoroastrians: Their Religious Beliefs and Practices.* London: Routledge and Kegan Paul, 1979.
A detailed examination of the historic development of the Zoroastrian beliefs over 3500 years. Recommended to those interested in the history of religious ideas. 295.'09'27.B69

Braunthal, Alfred. *Salvation and the Perfect Society: The Eternal Quest.* Amherst, MA: University of Massachusetts Press, 1979.
Braunthal believes that the non-secular, religious longing for salvation and the secular striving for a perfect society are prompted by the same basic needs and desires. In this book he traces the history of both approaches. 291.22.B73

*Enroth, Ronald. *The Lure of the Cults.* Chappaqua, New York: Christian Herald Books, 1979.
An up-to-date approach to the dynamics behind the success of many modern cults. Excellent. 301.5'8.EN7

Fry, C. George, and **James R. King.** *Islam: A Survey of Muslim Faith.* Grand Rapids: Baker Book House, 1980.
Believing that "no approach to Islam by Christians is possible until Christians grasp the genuine strengths of that religion," the authors describe all that is praiseworthy before comparing the teaching of Islam to Christianity. 297.4.F94

Hultkrantz, Ake. *The Religions of the American Indians.* Translated by M. Settersall. Berkeley, CA: University of California Press, 1979.
The first work in over a century to survey the complex religious beliefs and practices of the American Indians from the pre-literate period to the present. Treats their views of the supernatural, myths, rituals, etc. 299.7.H87

Johnson, Harry M., ed. *Religious Change and Continuity.* San Francisco: Jossey-Bass Publishers, 1979.
The growth of evangelical churches has attracted the attention of those who otherwise would not have considered religious movements worthy of consideration. The essays in this book, while manifesting naïveté about "born-again religion," do have a great deal to contribute concerning the "boom of quasi-religious cults" and Eastern mysticism. Stimulating reading. 290.J63

Leone, Mark P. *Roots of Modern Mormonism.* Cambridge, MA: Harvard University Press, 1979.
Traces the history of Mormonism from the

era of harassment to today's world of white collar workers and business executives.

301.58.L55

Morey, Robert A. *How to Answer a Jehovah's Witness.* Minneapolis: Bethany Fellowship, 1980.
Replete with photostatic copies of JW literature. Enables the reader to confront them when they come knocking on the front door.

289.9'2.M81

Noss, John Boyer. *Man's Religions.* 6th ed. New York: Macmillan Publishing Company, 1980.
Encyclopedic in scope, this work serves to introduce the busy reader to the whole range of religious beliefs and practices. Ideal for the pastor who wishes to remain well informed on these issues.   289.N84 1980

Parrinder, Edward Geoffrey. *Sex in the World's Religions.* New York: Oxford University Press, 1980.
A definitive study of sexology and religious belief in Indian, Buddhist, Chinese, Japanese, African, and Islamic traditions, together with an assessment of Hebrew and Christian beliefs. Revealing. Needs to be read in light of the Bible's teaching. A *must* for those engaged in the study of comparative religions.

291.21.P24

Raschke, Carl A. *The Interruption of Eternity: Modern Gnosticism and the Origins of the New Religious Consciousness.* Chicago: Nelson-Hall, 1980.
Traces modern religious movements to their early Gnostic beginnings. Describes their quest for inner truth and desire to escape from the temporal world. In describing the modern counterparts of early Gnosticism, Raschke relates its rise to the disaffection caused by the World and Asian wars, economic problems, and environmental difficulties.

291.R18

Robertson, Irvine. *What the Cults Believe.* 2d ed., revised. Chicago: Moody Press, 1979.
A former TEAM missionary, with extensive service in Asia, describes the rise, progress, and doctrinal distinctives of the major sects. Recommended for church libraries and those interested in deviant religious practices.

291.2.R54 1979

Scott, Latayne Colvett. *The Mormon Mirage.* Grand Rapids: Zondervan Publishing House, 1979.
Parallels William Schnell's bestselling book *Thirty Years a Watchtower Slave.* Contains the dramatic account of a young woman's entrapment in the LDS system, her conversion and exposé of Mormon doctrine. Breathes the air of authenticity.

289.3'092.S8

Sire, James W. *Scripture Twisting: Twenty Ways the Cults Misread the Bible.* Downers Grove, IL: InterVarsity Press, 1980.
Delves into the distortions and methods of deceit used by those who claim to be able to support their religious beliefs and/or practices with Scripture. Informative, enlightening, helpful.   291.2.S7

*****Tanner, Jerald,** and **Sandra Tanner.** *The Changing World of Mormonism.* Chicago: Moody Press, 1980.
Well written and ably documented, this work will take its place as the best treatment of the history and doctrinal development of Mormonism available today.   289.3.T15

Wilson, Howard A. *Invasion From the East.* Minneapolis: Augsburg Publishing House, 1979.
Evaluates the impact of Eastern religions on Western society and culture. Voices justifiable concern over the spiritual barrenness which has made America vulnerable to such inroads. Sobering.   261.2.W69

AUTHOR
INDEX

A

Achtemeier, Elizabeth, 55
Achtemeier, Paul. J., 5
Ackerman, Paul R., 39
Adams, Jay Edward, 7, 47, 52
Adeney, Walter Frederick, 11
Aharoni, Yohanan, 7
Aland, Kurt, 15
Alexander, Joseph Addison, 17
Alexander, Olive J., 39
Alexander, William Menzies, 30
Alford, Henry, 11
Allen, Charles Livingstone, 59
Ames, Louis Bates, 39
Andersen, Francis Ian, 13
Anderson, Bernhard, W., 7
Anderson, David A., 1
Anderson, G. W., 9
Anderson, Robert, 29, 30
Anderson, Robert Maples, 65
Archer, Gleason Leonard, Jr., 2
Armerding, George D., 7
Armerding, Hudson T., 51
Armstrong, Ben, 47
Arnold, William V., 39
Arrington, Leonard J., 65
Augsburger, David, 34, 39
Ausubel, David P., 34
Ayling, Stanley, 62

B

Bailey, Lloyd R., 30
Bailey, Mary Frances, 49
Bailey, Robert W., 49, 52
Bainton, Roland Herbert, 61
Bakan, David, 39
Baker, William H., 52
Banks, Robert, 47

Barber, Aldyth Ayleen, 39
Barber, Cyril John, 18, 39
Barnes, Albert, 27
Baron, David, 7
Barth, Karl, 25
Bartlett, John, 2
Battles, Ford Lewis, 25
Bauer, Walter, 2
Baughen, Michael, 51
Bavinck, Herman, 5
Baxter, Batsell Barrett, 7
Baxter, James Sidlon, 65
Beauchamp, T. L., 33
Bebbington, David W., 61
Becker, Joachim, 9
Berkhof, Hendrikus, 25
Bernard, John Henry, 19
Bernstein, Burton, 9
Bitton, Davis, 65
Blackwell, Muriel F., 40
Blackwell, William L., 40
Blanch, Stuart, 9
Blitchington, W. Peter, 40
Bloesch, Donald G., 34
Boice, James Montgomery, 21, 29, 30
Bonar, Horatius, 11
Bonhoeffer, Dietrich, 26
Bopp, Stephen G., 60
Bosch, David J., 57
Bossant, Donald E., 59
Botterwick, G. Johannes, 1
Bowie, Norman E., 33
Boyce, Mary, 65
Boys, Mary C., 59
Brand, Paul, 29
Braunthal, Alfred, 65
Bray, Gerald Lewis, 29
Brekke, Milo L., 49
Bridges, Charles, 13

Bridges, William, 40
Broderick, Carlfred, 40
Bromiley, Geoffrey William, 1, 25, 40, 47
Brown, John, 21
Brown, Raymond E., 18
Brown, Raymond Kay, 52
Bruce, Alexander Balmain, 16, 22
Bruce, Frederick Fyvie, 18, 19, 27, 62
Buell, Jon A., 28
Bullinger, Ethelbert William, 22, 28
Bullock, C. Hassell, 13
Burgon, John William, 15
Burkhardt, Helmut, 29
Burnett, Linda, 43
Bush, L. Russ, 6
Butterfield, Herbert, 61

C

Calvin, John, 5
Candlish, Robert Smith, 11, 22
Cannon, J. R., 52
Carkhuff, Robert R., 52
Carlson, C. C., 46
Carroll, Benajah Harvey, 6
Carson, David A., 15, 18
Carter, John Daniel, 52
Cartlidge, David R., 16
Catherwood, Henry Frederick Ross, 33
Cavanagh, Michael E., 34
Cedar, Paul A., 34
Chamberlain, William Douglas, 15
Charnock, Stephen, 27
Chase, Joan Ames, 39
Chelune, Gordon J., 34
Cherry, Conrad, 26

Chesser, Barbara, 45
Childs, Brevard S., 9
Church, F. F., 61
Church, T. George, 61
Clark, Clifford E., 62
Clark, Stephen B., 40
Clarke, Arthur G., 13
Clements, Ronald Ernest, 13
Clements, William M., 52
Clinebell, Howard John, 53
Clines, David J. A., 11
Cochrane, Donald B., 59
Coleman, Lucien E., Jr., 5
Coleman, Richard J., 26
Coleman, Robert Emerson, 22
Coleman, William L., 53
Collier, Kenneth W., 35
Collins, Gary R., 34, 53
Conger, John Janeway, 43
Conway, Sally, 40
Coote, Robert B., 13
Coote, Robert T., 53
Cosgrove, Francis M., Jr., 51
Cosgrove, Mark P., 53
Court, John M., 22
Cowan, George M., 57
Cox, Jimmie, 44
Cox-Gedmark, Jan, 34
Crane, Thomas E., 34
Cranfield, Charles E. B., 19
Criswell, Wallie Amos, 47
Crouwel, J. H., 10
Cully, Iris V., 40
Culver, Robert Duncan, 14
Custance, Arthur C., 7, 26

D

Daane, James, 55
Dallimore, Arnold A., 63
Davidson, Robert, 11
Davies, G. I., 11
Davis, James Hill, 47
Davis, John D., 11
Davis, John James, 11
Dayton, Edward R., 50
DeFain, John, 45
Deissmann, Gustav Adolf, 15
Delitzsch, Franz Julius, 9
Demaray, Donald E., 55
Demarest, Gary W., 19
Deweese, Charles W., 51
Dickson, David, 13
DiGiacomo, James J., 33
Dittes, James E., 49
Dobson, James Clayton, Jr., 34, 40
Dodd, Charles Harold, 55
Doig, Desmond, 63
Dollar, Truman E., 40
Donovan, Peter, 7
Douglas, J. D., 1
Drakeford, John W., 40
Drescher, John M., 41
Drewery, Mary, 63
Driggers, B. Carlisle, 49
Drucker, Peter Ferdinand, 51

Dryness, William, 9
Duncan, Homer, 26
Dungan, David L., 16
Dunker, Marilee Pierce, 63

E

Eck, John, 61
Edwards, David L., 61
Edwards, Thomas Charles, 19
Efird, James M., 14
Ehrlich, Eugene, 3
Eichhorn, David Max, 50
Elder, Betty Doak, 42
Ellison, Craig W., 41
Ellison, Henry Leopold, 7
Ellul, Jacques, 61
Engel, James F., 47
Enroth, Ronald, 65
Ericson, Edward E., Jr., 63
Ericson, Edward E., Jr., 63
Erickson, Millard J., 29
Evans, Donald, 33

F

Fairbairn, Patrick, 8, 14, 19
Fairchild, Roy W., 53
Falk, Peter, 57
Faricy, Robert, 35
Faul, John, 34
Feigenberg, Loma, 53
Feinberg, Charles Lee, 8, 30
Feinberg, Paul David, 26
Finegan, Jack, 8
Finney, Charles Grandison, 35
Fisher, Wallace E., 55
Flynn, Leslie B., 11
Foh, Susan T., 8
Ford, D. W. Cleverley, 56
Ford, Desmond, 14
Fordyce, Jack K., 51
Forell, George Wolfgang, 33
Forsyth, Peter Taylor, 56
Freedman, David Noel, 13
Freeman, Carroll B., 41
Fretz, Bruce R., 53
Fry, C. George, 65
Fuller, Daniel P., 26
Fuller, Reginald Horace, 56

G

Gallup, George, Jr., 47
Gaylin, Willard, 35
Geisler, Norman Leo, 6, 26
Getz, Gene A., 41, 50
Gillespie, Virgil Bailey, 29
Girard, Robert C., 47
Glasser, William, 35
Glickman, S. Craig, 35
Gloag, Paton James, 18
Godet, Frederic Louis, 18
Gottman, John Mordecai, 41
Goudge, William, 22
Goulder, Michael, 28
Govett, Robert, 30

Gratsch, Edward J., 25
Gray, John, 30
Greaves, Richard L., 25
Green, Edward Michael Bankes, 29
Green, William Henry, 9, 11
Gromacki, Robert Glenn, 20
Groome, Thomas H., 59
Grunlan, Stephen A., 57
Gundry, Patricia, 41
Gundry, Stanley N., 26
Gunn, David M., 11

H

Habblewaite, Brian, 57
Habermas, Gary R., 28
Hagner, Donald A., 17
Hale, James Russell, 47
Hals, Ronald M., 8
Halverson, Kaye, 41
Hamilton, Michael Pollock, 53
Hamm, Cornel M., 59
Hancock, Maxine, 41
Hanna, Mark M., 26
Harcum, Eugene Rae, 41
Hardesty, Nancy A., 63
Hardy, Alister, 29
Harris, Murray J., 17
Harris, Robert Laird, 2
Harrison, Roland Kenneth, 12
Hart, Arthur Fenton, 15
Hass, Aaron, 41
Hatch, Nathan O., 49
Hauck, Paul A., 53
Hazelip, Harold, 7
Headington, Bonnie Joy, 53
Heim, Pamela, 42
Hendricks, Jeanne W., 41
Hendriksen, William, 20
Hengel, Martin, 18, 61
Hengstenberg, Ernst Wilhelm, 18
Henry, Carl Ferdin, 26
Henry, Howard, 26
Henslin, James M., 42
Herron, Orley, 42
Hess, Karen M., 41
Hesselgrave, David J., 48, 57
Hick, John, 57
Hiebert, William J., 55
Hill, David, 17
Hiltner, Seward, 48, 49, 54
Hindson, Edward E., 14, 42
Hiscox, Edward T., 62
Hodge, Archibald A., 6
Hodge, Charles, 20
Hoekstra, Harvey Thomas, 50
Hoeldtke, Clyde, 52
Hoffman, John Charles, 54
Holmes, Deborah Lott, 42
Hook, H. Philip, 27
Hopkins, C. Howard, 63
Hort, Fenton John Anthony, 15, 62
Houlden, James Leslie, 20
Houston, James M., 27
Howard, George, 20

Howard, Ted, 62
Hromas, R. P., 5
Huffman, John A., Jr., 12
Hughes, Graham, 22
Hulme, William Edward, 54
Hultgren, Arland J., 18
Hultkrantz, Ake, 65
Hunt, James G., 51
Hunter, Archibald Macbride, 28
Hunter, George G., III, 48
Hunter, Ian, 63
Hyatt, James Philip, 12
Hyder, O. Quentin, 28

I

Ilg, Frances L., 39
Inmon, Marvin N., 46
Irion, Paul E., 48
Ishida, Tomoo, 9

J

Jacobson, Neil S., 54
Jensen, Gordon D., 42
Jewett, Robert, 20, 30
Johnson, Harry M., 65
Johnson, Paul, 44
Johnson, Samuel, 56
Johnson, Samuel Lewis, Jr., 6
Johnston, Olaf Raymond, 42
Johnston, Robert K., 50
Jourard, Sidney M., 35
Julien, Tom, 12

K

Kagan, Jerome, 43
Kalish, Richard A., 35
Kane, J. Herbert, 57
Kantzer, Kenneth S., 26
Kappelman, Murray M., 39
Käsemann, Ernst, 20
Kasper, Walter, 42
Kazepides, Anastasios C., 59
Keck, Leander E., 20
Kelly, Robert K., 42
Kelly, William, 14
Kelsey, Morton T., 31
Kendall, Earline Doak, 42
Kerr, Horace L., 54
Ketterman, Grace H., 40
Kidner, Derek, 12
King, James R., 65
Kirk, J. Andrew, 57
Kissinger, Warren S., 17
Kistemaker, Simon J., 16, 17
Kitchen, Kenneth Anderson, 8
Klimek, David, 42
Klotsche, E. H., 25
Knight, Bryan M., 42
Knight, George W., III, 20
Koop, C. Everett, 36
Kopp, Ruth Lewshenia, 54
Korthals, Richard G., 50
Koteskey, Ronald L., 54
Kroll, Woodrow Michael, 56

Kurtz, Johann Heinrich, 10
Kutash, Irwin L., 54

L

La Haye, Timothy F., 35
Lamm, Maurice, 43
Lande, Nathaniel, 33
Larson, Lars L., 51
Laws, Sophie, 22
Lee, Francis Nigel, 35
Lee, Mark W., 43
Leon-Dufour, Xavier, 2
Leone, Mark P., 65
Leslie, Robert C., 54
Lewis, Arthur H., 12
Lewis, Gregg A., 43
Lewis, Margaret M., 43
Liddon, Henry Parry, 28
Lieberman, Morton A., 54
Lightfoot, John, 2
Lightfoot, Joseph Barber, 15, 20
Lindgren, Alvin J., 50
Linn, Dennis, 54
Linn, Mary Jane, 54
Linn, Matthew, 54
Linthorst, Ann Tremaine, 43
Littauer, M. A., 10
Lloyd–Jones, David Martyn, 21
Loader, J. A., 13
Lockerbie, D. Bruce, 5, 59
Lovelace, Richard F., 35
Lucas, R. C., 21
Ludwig, David J., 43
Lynn, Robert W., 59

M

MacArthur, John F., Jr., 6, 18
Mace, David Robert, 49
Mace, Vera, 49
MacKay, Donald M., 29
Maier, John R., 5
Mare, W. Harold, 15
Margolin, Gayla, 54
Martin, Ralph Philip, 48
Matheny, Kenneth B., 54
Mattson, Elsie, 43
Mattson, Lloyd, 43
Mayers, Marvin K., 57
Mayfield, James L., 43
Mays, James Luther, 16
McCarther, P. Kyle, Jr., 12
McDill, Wayne, 50
McDonald, Hugh Dermot, 6, 21
McDowell, Josh, 26
McGavran, Donald Anderson, 48, 57
McKim, Donald K., 6
McKinley, Edward H., 62
McKinley, John, 35
McMahon, J. J., 35
Meier, Paul D., 43
Meier, Richard, 43
Meredith, Donald, 43
Meyer, Heinrich August Wilhelm, 2

Miller, Randolph Crump, 59
Milligan, George, 21
Milligan, William, 28
Mills, David H., 53
Minirth, Frank, 43
Morey, Robert A., 66
Morrison, Frederick J., 42
Morrison, George H., 18
Moule, Charles Francis Digby, 28
Moule, Handley Carr Glyn, 28
Murphey, Cecil, 35
Murphy, James Gracey, 12
Murray, Lawrence L., 59
Mussen, Paul Henry, 43
Myerhoff, Barbara, 46
Mylander, Charles, 48

N

Narramore, Stanley Bruce, 43, 52
Nathansen, Bernard N., 35
Neal, Daniel, 62
Needham, David C., 36
Neil, William, 10
Nestle, E., 15
Nettles, Tom J., 6
Niesel, Wilhelm, 25
Noll, Mark A., 49
Norman, William H., 55
Noss, John Boyer, 66

O

Oden, Thomas C., 26
Ogden, Schubert Miles, 55
Olivier, Daniel A. A., 63
Olson, Robert Wallace, 50
Orr, James, 28
Osborne, Cecil G., 36
Osgood, Donald W., 36
Ostling, Richard N., 35
Owens, Virginia Stem, 36

P

Packer, James Innell, 6, 29, 36
Parker, Mildred, 59
Parkinson, Cycil Northcote, 51
Parrinder, Edward Geoffrey, 66
Pentecost, John Dwight, 19
Perez, Joseph Francis, 55
Perry, Lloyd Merle, 56
Peters, George Nathaniel Henry, 31
Peterson, Eugene H., 36
Pickering, Ernest, 48
Pierce, R. M., 52
Pierson, Robert H., 36
Pink, Arthur Walkington, 30
Pinson, W. M., Jr., 33
Pippert, Rebecca Manley, 51
Plekker, Robert J., 44
Plummer, Alfred, 22
Poling, David, 47
Powell, John, 36
Powers, Bruce P., 36
Prochnow, Herbert V., 56

Prochnow, Herbert V., Jr., 56
Puryear, Douglas A., 55

R

Rad, Gerhard von, 10
Radmacher, Earl D., 6
Raines, Robert A., 48
Raleigh, Alexander, 12
Ramsden, William E., 58
Ramsey, William Mitchell, 17
Raschke, Carl A., 66
Raven, John Howard, 10
Rayburn, Robert G., 48
Reid, Helen F., 53
Rice, David G., 44
Richards, Lawrence O., 44, 51, 52
Ricoeur, Paul, 6
Rienecher, Fritz, 16
Rifkin, Jeremy, 62
Ringgren, Helmer, 1
Riordan, Richard J., 54
Roberts, Betty Holroyd, 44
Robertson, Irvine, 66
Robinson, Haddon W., 56
Robinson, Henry Wheeler, 8
Robinson, James, 44
Robinson, John Arthur Thomas, 21, 31
Rogers, Jack B., 6
Rogerson, J. W., 10
Rokeach, Milton, 36
Roleder, George, 44
Ross, Charlotte, 50
Rowatt, G. Wade, 44
Rowatt, Mary Jo, 44
Rowley, Harold Henry, 13
Rubin, Lillian B., 44
Rudnick, Milton L., 33
Rychlak, Joseph F., 36
Ryrie, Charles Caldwell, 6, 8

S

Sabourin, Leopold, 6
Sainsburg, R. M., 63
Sampley, J. Paul, 17
Sandmel, Samuel, 21
Santa, George F., 13
Sasson, Jack M., 12
Saul, Leon J., 44
Scaramella, Thomas J., 55
Schaeffer, Francis August, 36
Schaller, Lyle E., 52
Schlesinger, Louis B., 54
Schmidt, Paul F., 55
Schultz, Samuel J., 10
Schwartz, Leonard J., 44
Schwartz, Roslyn, 44
Schweizer, Edward, 28
Scott, Latayne Colvett, 66
Seligman, Linda, 55
Shannon, Thomas A., 33
Sharma, Prakash C., 45
Shawchuck, Norman, 50
Shedd, William Greenough Thayer, 31
Simcox, William Henry, 16, 17
Simmons, Paul D., 33

Simons, Joseph, 45
Sire, James W., 66
Slade, Afton, 33
Slonaker, David F., 45
Small, Dwight Hervey, 45
Smart, James D., 8
Smeaton, George, 28
Smith, Barth, 52
Smith, Harold Ivan, 45
Smith, Harold T., 52
Smith, Warren Thomas, 63
Snyder, Howard A., 63
Sorenson, Stephen, 54
Sponheim, Paul R., 27
Spray, Pauline E., 45
Stahmann, Robert F., 55
Stanley, Arthur Peurhyn, 21
Stater, Peter, 27
Stedman, Ray C., 22, 48
Stendahl, Brita, 33
Stephens, Shirley, 17
Steven, Hugh, 58
Stevens, Edward, 33
Stewart, Charles William, 55
Stier, Rudolf, 22
Stinett, Nick, 45
Stollak, Gary E., 45
Stott, John Robert Walmsey, 5, 21, 36, 53
Strauss, Lehman, 31
Strauss, Richard L., 37
Strommen, Merton P., 49
Strubbar, John R., 56
Sweet, John Philip McMurdo, 23
Swindoll, Charles Rozell, 37, 45

T

Tan, Paul Lee, 56
Tanner, Jerald, 66
Tanner, Sandra, 66
Tatford, Frederick Albert, 14
Taylor, Thomas, 21
Tenney, Merrill Chapin, 28, 37
Thatcher, Floyd, 45
Thatcher, Harriett, 45
Thayer, Lee, 34
Thiessen, Henry Clarence, 25
Thiselton, Anthony C., 16
Thomas, David M., 45
Thompson, John Arthur, 14
Tollers, Vincent L., 5
Toon, Peter, 27, 28, 62
Toussaint, Stanley Dale, 19
Travis, Patricia Y., 46
Travis, Robert P., 46
Travis, Stephen H., 31
Tufte, Virginia, 46
Turnbull, Ralph G., 50
Turner, Nigel, 16

U

Unger, Merrill F., 2

V

Van Kaam, Adrian, 37
Vander Lugt, Herbert, 30

Vernon, Robert, 46
Vos, Geerhardus, 31
Voshell, Dorothy, 46

W

Walchenbach, John, 25
Waltke, Bruce Kenneth, 2
Walrath, Douglas Alan, 48
Walvoord, John Flipse, 31
Ward, Ted, 46
Warfield, Benjamin B., 6
Warlick, Harold C., Jr., 37
Warns, Johannes, 48
Warren, Thomas B., 46
Watson, David, 48
Webber, Robert E., 27
Weber, Timothy P., 31
Weil, Raymond, 51
Wells, William W., 62
Wenham, Gordon J., 12
Wesley, Charles, 64
Wessler, Richard L., 37
Wessler, Ruth A., 37
Westcott, Brooke Foss, 8, 17, 21
Westermann, Claus, 13
Whitcomb, John Clement, Jr., 11, 12
White, James F., 51
White, Reginald Ernest Oscar, 8, 19, 28
White, William, 15
White, William Jr., 2, 64
White, Woodie W., 47
Whitehead, Evelyn Eaton, 37
Whitehead, James D., 37
Whitelam, Keith W., 10
Wiersbe, Warren W., 30, 56
Wilcock, Michael, 19
Wilke, Harold H., 49
Williams, Dorothy L., 49
Willimon, William H., 56
Willis, Wesley, R., 60
Wilson, Howard A., 66
Wilson, J. Christy, Jr., 51
Wilson, John Oliver, 37
Wilson, Robert Leroy, 56
Wise, Jonathan Kurland, 37
Wise, Susan Kierr, 37
Wood, Leon J., 10
Woodbridge, John D., 49
Workman, Herbert B., 62
Wright, Charles Henry Hamilton, 14
Wright, H. Elliot, 59
Wright, Harry Norman, 46
Wright, J. Stafford, 1
Würthwein, Ernest, 10

Y

Yamauchi, Edwin M., 17
Yancey, Philip, 29

Z

Zaccaria, Joseph S., 60

TITLE INDEX

A

Aborting America, 35
Acts and History of Earliest Christianity, 18
Administrative Manager, 52
Adolescence Is Not an Illness, 43
After Affluence, 37
Afterlife, 31
Afternoon: For Women at the Heart of Life, 41
Agape Evangelism, 50
Agenda for Theology, 26
Aging and Communications, 45
All the Trees and Woody Plants of the Bible, 1
Amos Among the Prophets, 13
Analysis of the Institutes of the Christian Religion of John Calvin, 25
Analytical Studies in the Psalms, 13
Anchor Bible: I Samuel, 12
Anchor Bible: Hosea, 13
Answer Is the Spirit, 28
Anthropology and the Old Testament, 10
Antichrist, The, 30
Apostolic Preaching and Its Developments, 55
Approach to Christian Ethics, 33
Approaches to Guidance in Contemporary Education, 60
Archaeological History of the Ancient Middle East, 8
Archaeology of New Testament Cities in Western Asia Minor, 17
Art of Creative Thinking, 50
Art of Helping, 52

Art of Married Love, 42
Ascension of Christ, 28
Asking Questions, 5
Assessment in Developmental Career Counseling, 55
Atonement, The, 27
Augustine: His Life and Thought, 63
Authority and Interpretation of the Bible, 6
Autumn Years, 45
Awakening to God, 29

B

Baptism: Studies in the Original Christian Baptism, 48
Baptists and the Bible, 6
Battle for the Mind, 35
Becoming a Couple, 44
Becoming One, 43
Behold the King, 19
Beneath Mate Selection and Marriage, 42
Best Is Yet to Come, 8
Betrayal of the West, 61
Between You and You, 35
Beyond Assertiveness, 34
Beyond the Battle for the Bible, 36
Bible and Christ, 6
Bible in Its Literary Milieu: Contemporary Essays, 5
Bible in Its World, 8
Bible in the Church, 8
Bible Studies, 15
Biblical Doctrine of Regeneration, 29
Biblical Doctrine of the Reign of God, 30

Biblical Essays, 15
Biblical Ethics, 8
Biblical Interpretation in Religious Education, 59
Biblical Perspectives on Death, 30
Biblical Preaching, 56
Biblical Separation, 48
Birth of Christ, 28
Birthright: Christian Do You Know Who You Are?, 36
Big Little School, 59
Body Life, 48
Book of Esther, 12
Book of Genesis and Part of the Book of Exodus, 11
Book of Jeremiah, 14
Book of Leviticus, 12
Brethren, Hang Together, 47
Brief Counseling with RET, 53
Building Family Strengths, 45
Business Ethics, 33

C

Can We Trust the Bible?, 6
Can We Trust the Old Testament?, 10
Care and Counseling of the Aging, 52
Career Guide to Professional Associations, 49
Caring Enough to Confront, 39
Celluloid Persuasion, 59
Central Significance of Culture, 35
Changing Images of the Family, 46
Changing World of Mormonism, 66
Child: An Introduction to Developmental Psychology, 42

Child Development and Personality, 43
Childhood Emotional Pattern and Maturity, 44
Childhood Emotional Pattern in Marriage, 44
Children of Promise, 47
Christ and the Kingdom, 28
Christ the Center, 26
Christian Child Development, 40
Christian Counseling, 53
Christian England, 61
Christian Ethics for Today, 33
Christian Faith, 25
Christian Hope and the Future, 31
Christian Leadership, 36
Christian Life Patterns, 37
Christian Religious Education, 59
Christian Shepherd, 48
Christian Words, 16
Christianity and Other Religions, 57
Chronology of Paul's Life, 20
Church Growth, 48
Church in a Changing Society, 58
Colossians: The Mystery of Christ in Us, 19
Commentaries, 5
Commentary on Colossians and Philemon, 21
Commentary on Hebrews, Exegetical and Expository, 22
Commentary on James, 22
Commentary on John's Gospel, 18
Commentary on Romans, 20
Commentary on the Acts of the Apostles, 17
Commentary on the Epistle of James, 22
Commentary on the First Epistle to the Corinthians, 19
Commentary on the Gospel of Mark, 17
Commentary on the Gospel of St. John, 18
Commentary on the New Testament, 2
Commentary on the New Testament from the Talmud and Hebraica, 2
Commentary on the Psalms, 13
Communication in the Counseling Relationship, 53
Community of the Beloved Disciple, 18
Complete Woman, The, 41
Computer–Konkordanz zum Novum Testamentum Graece, 2
Conquering Loneliness, 37
Contemporary Christian Communications, 47
Contemporary Growth Therapies, 53
Continuity and Discontinuity in Church History, 61
Coping with Difficult People, 55
Coping with Physical Disability, 34

Coping with Stress in the Minister's Home, 49
Corporate Personality in Ancient Israel, 8
Couples: How to Confront Problems and Maintain Loving Relationships, 40
Courtship, Marriage, and the Family, 42
Creating a Caring Congregation, 49
Creative Conflict in Religious Education and Church Administration, 59
Creative Preaching, 55
Criswell's Guidebook for Pastors, 47
Critical and Exegetical Commentary on the Acts of the Apostles, 18
Critical and Exegetical Commentary on the Book of Exodus, 12
Critical and Exegetical Commentary on the Epistle to the Romans, 19
Crosscurrents in Leadership, 51
Crucial Questions in Apologetics, 26
Cultural Anthropology, 57

D

Daniel, 14
Daniel and His Prophecy, 14
Death and the Caring Community, 44
Demonic Possession in the New Testament, 30
Developing Spiritually Sensitive Children, 39
Devotional Guide to Biblical Lands, 7
Dictionary of the New Testament, 2
Discourses upon the Existence and Attributes of God, 27
Discovering Free Will and Personal Responsibility, 36
Divine Healing of the Body, 65
Divorce and the Christian, 44
Doctrine of Endless Punishment, 31
Doctrine of the Atonement as Taught by Christ Himself, 28
Doctrine of the Word of God, 25
Documents for the Study of the Gospels, 16
Domain of Moral Education, 59
Don't Push Your Preschooler, 39
Down to Earth, 53
Dual–Career Marriage, 44
Dynamics of Religion, 27
Dynamics of Spiritual Life, 35

E

Effective Parent, 40

Electric Church, 47
Emerging Order, 62
Emerging Role of Deacons, 51
Emotions: Can You Trust Them?, 34
Enchiridion of Commonplaces Against Luther and Other Enemies of the Church, 61
Encounter with Terminal Illness, 54
Encyclopedia of 7,700 Illustrations, 56
Enjoying Single Parenthood, 42
Entrance into the Kingdom, 30
Epistle to the Hebrews, 22
Epistles of John, 21
Epistles of St. John, 22
Epistles of St. Paul to the Corinthians, 21
Essays on Biblical Interpretation, 6
Essentials of Discipleship, 51
Esther: The Triumph of God's Sovereignty, 12
Ethical Confrontation in Counseling, 54
Ethical Theory and Business, 33
Ethics, Morality and the Media, 34
Evangelical Theology, 62
Evangelicals at an Impasse, 50
Evangelistic Preaching, 56
Evangelizing the American Jew, 50
Evidence That Demands a Verdict, 26
Exegetical Grammar of the Greek New Testament, 15
Exodus, 12
Exploring Human Values, 35
Exposition of Ezekiel, 14
Exposition of Paul's Epistle to the Romans, 20
Exposition of the Book of Isaiah, 14
Exposition of the First Epistle to the Corinthians, 20
Exposition of the Second Epistle to the Corinthians, 20
Exposition of Titus, 21
Expository and Exegetical Studies, 15
Expository Studies in I John, 22
Ezra and Nehemiah, 11
Ezra and Nehemiah, An Introduction and Commentary, 12

F

Faith and Freedom, 55
Faith and Process, 27
Faith for the Nonreligious, 29
Faithful Sayings in the Pastoral Letters, 20
Familiar Quotations, 2
Family and the Fellowship, 48
Family Counseling, 55
Family Foundations, 43

Family Life and the Church, 45
Farewell Discourse and Final Prayer of Jesus, 18
Fearfully and Wonderfully Made, 29
Feelings: Our Vital Signs, 35
Finding Hope Again, 53
First and Second Corinthians, 19
First Epistle of John, 22
First New Testament, 15
First Things First, 33
Flood: Local or Global, 7
Focus on Christ, 36
Forever Principle, 41
Forgotten Truths, 30
Fragance of the Lord, 7
Free to Obey, 27
From Babylon to Bethlehem, 7
Fullness and Freedom, 21
Funeral and the Mourners, 48

G

General Introduction to the Old Testament, 9
General Survey of the History of the Canon of the New Testament, 17
Genesis and Semitic Tradition, 11
Genesis 12–50, 11
Genius of Paul, 21
George Whitefield, 63
Gesell Institute's Child from One to Six, 39
Gift of Love, 43
Giver and His Gifts, 28
God and History, 30
God and Marriage, 40
God at Work in Israel, 10
God Has Spoken, 6
God Here and Now, 27
God Still Speaks, 27
God Who Speaks and Shows, 26
God's New Society, 21
God's Plan in All the Ages, 30
Gospel According to Matthew, 17
Gospel and Law, 26
Gospel in America, 49
Gospels in Current Study, 16
Grace and Faith in the Old Testament, 8
Great Cloud of Witnesses in Hebrews Eleven, 22
Great Women of Faith, 63
Greek New Testament, 15
Greek–English Lexicon of the New Testament and Other Early Christian Literature, 2
Group Development Through Participation Training, 35
Growth Counseling, 53
Growth of the Church in Africa, 57

H

Handbook on Stress and Anxiety, 54

Healing Life's Hurts, 54
Healing the Dying, 54
Hebrews and Hermeneutics, 22
Heirs Together, 41
Helping People in Crisis, 55
Henry Ward Beecher, 62
Historical Geography of Asia Minor, 17
Histories and Prophecies of Daniel, 14
History of Christian Doctrine, 25
History of Christian Ethics, 33
History of Israel from Conquest to Exile, 11
History of the Puritans, 62
History of the Religion of Israel, 10
Holiness and the Will of God, 29
Holy Spirit, 28
Holy Spirit, The, 28
Home: Where Life Makes Up Its Mind, 45
Hospice Handbook, 53
How Should I Love You?, 45
How to Answer a Jehovah's Witness, 66
How to Become a Successful Christian Leader, 36
How to Have a Good Marriage Before and After the Wedding, 43
How to Increase Your Sunday School Attendance, 59
How to Minister to Senior Adults in Your Church, 54
How to Start Counseling, 54
How to Teach the Bible, 5
Human Science and Human Dignity, 29
Hurting Parent, 43

I

I Believe in the Church, 48
I Believe in the Creator, 27
Illustrated Bible Dictionary, 1
In Retrospect: Remembrance of Things Past, 62
In Search of a Father, 44
Incarnation and Myth, 28
Indexes of the Doorway Papers, 7
Inerrancy, 6
Inspiration, 6
Inspiration of Scripture, 5
Inspiration of the Bible, 6
Integration of Psychology and Theology, 52
International Standard Bible Encyclopedia, 1
Interpreting Religious Experience, 7
Interpreting the Gospel, 16
Interruption of Eternity, 66
Introduction to Bioethics, 33
Introduction to Christian Worship, 51

Introduction to Philosophy, 26
Introduction to the Old Testament as Scripture, 9
Introduction to the Poetic Books of the Old Testament, 13
Introduction to the Theology of Karl Barth, 25
Invasion from the East, 66
Isaiah 1–39, 13
Isaiah's Immanuel, 14
Islam: A Survey of Muslim Faith, 65
Israel at the Center of History and Revelation, 8
Israel's United Monarchy, 10
Issues in Christian Ethics, 33
Issues of Theological Conflict, 26

J

Jeremiah: Prophet Under Siege, 14
Jesus: God, Ghost or Guru?, 28
Jesus Against the Rapture, 30
Jesus and His Adversaries, 18
Jesus and His Coming, 31
Jesus Christ is Lord, 28
Jewish Way in Love and Marriage, 43
Jews, Greeks, and Barbarians, 61
Job, 13
John, 19
John R. Mott, 63
John Wesley, 62
Joseph: God's Man in Egypt, 11
Journal of Charles Wesley, 64
Joy of Caring, 34
Judges/Ruth, 12
Judiastic Christianity, 62
Just King: Monarchical Judicial Authority in Ancient Israel, 10

K

King James Version Debate, 15
Kingdom Living Here and Now, 18
Knowing Christ, 35
Knowing Man, 29

L

Land of the Bible, 7
Language of the New Testament, 16
Leadership, 51
Leading Churches Through Change, 48
Lectures in Systematic Theology, 25
Let My People Go, 50
Leviticus, an Introduction and Commentary, 12
Liberating Limits, 12
Liberation Theology, 57
Licensing and Certification of Psychologists and Counselors, 53

Life and Work on the Mission Field, 57
Linguistic Key to the Greek New Testament, 16
Listening to the Giants, 56
Living Creatively, 37
Living in the Shadow of the Second Coming, 31
Living Together, 45
Living Word of the Bible, 7
Loneliness: The Search for Intimacy, 41
Long Obedience in the Same Direction, 36
Long Term Marriage, 45
Loving One Another, 50
Luke, 18
Lure of the Cults, 65

M

Make Your Tomorrow Better, 34
Making Friends for Christ, 50
Malcolm Muggeridge, 63
Man and Woman in Christ, 40
Man of Vision; Woman of Prayer, 63
Man's Religions, 66
Managing in Turbulent Times, 51
Managing with People, 51
Marching to Glory, 62
Marital Interaction, 41
Marital Therapy, 54
Mark, 18
Marriage: How to Keep a Good Thing Growing, 40
Marriage and Family in a Changing Society, 42
Marriage, Divorce and Remarriage in the Bible, 7
Marriage Means Encounter, 44
Married Man, 46
Mastering New Testament Greek, 15
Matthew, 18
Measure of a Marriage, 41
Messianic Expectation in the Old Testament, 9
Mid–Life Developmental and Clinical Issues, 55
Middle-Aged Career Dropouts, 44
Millennialism, 30
Mind of Matthew, 19
Minister as Family Counselor, 55
Minister's Opportunities, 50
Ministering to the Grieving, 52
Ministry of the Word, 56
Ministry with the Aging, 52
Miracles of Christ, 16
Models of Metropolitan Ministry, 49
Modern Study in the Book of Proverbs, 13
More Than Redemption, 52
Mormon Experience, 65
Mormon Mirage, 66
Moses Principle, 51

Mother Teresa: Her People and Her Word, 63
Multiple Staff and the Larger Church, 52
Mysterious Matter of Mind, 7
Myth and History in the Book of Revelation, 22

N

Nature and Religious Imagination, 26
Nelson's Expository Dictionary of the Old Testament, 2
Never Touch a Tiger, 58
New Horizons in World Mission, 57
New King James Bible New Testament, 16
New Life in the Church, 48
New Life: Readings in Christian Theology, 29
New Testament Prophecy, 17
New Testament View of Women, 17
Notes on the Epistles of St. Paul, 20
Novum Testament Graece, 15

O

O Come, Let Us Worship, 48
Old Testament History of Redemption, 9
Old Testament in the New, 6
Old Testament Speaks, 10
Out of the Salt–Shaker and Into the World, 51
Overeaters: Eating Styles and Personality, 37
Oxford American Dictionary, 3

P

Parables of Christ, 16
Parables of Jesus, 17
Parables of Jesus: A History of Interpretation and Bibliography, 17
Parkinson: The Law, 51
Part of Me Is Missing, 45
Parting Counsels, 21
Passport to the Bible, 5
Past, Present, and Future of Biblical Theology, 8
Pastor's Handbook of Church Management, 52
Pastoral Epistles, 19
Pastoral Epistles, 19
Patterns in History, 61
Patterns of Biblical Spirituality, 34
Paul: Crisis in Galatia, 20
Paul and His Letters, 20
Paul's Idea of Community, 47
Paul's Letters from Prison, 20
Pauline Eschatology, 31
Pauline Partnership in Christ, 17

Pauline Studies, 17
Persecution in the Early Church, 62
Perspectives on Evangelical Theology, 26
Peter, Stephen, James, and John: Studies in Early Non–Pauline Christianity, 18
Philosophy of Revelation, 5
Planning Strategies for World Evangelization, 50
Planting Churches Cross Culturally, 48
Polar Structures in the Book of Qohlet, 13
Positive Preaching and the Modern Mind, 56
Prayerobics, 35
Praying for Inner Healing, 35
Preaching and Worship in the Small Church, 56
Preaching with Confidence, 55
Preface to Pastoral Theology, 49
Premarital Counseling, 55
Preparing For Parenthood, 46
Prescription for Preaching, 56
Pressure Points, 36
Principles and Practice of Rational–Emotive Therapy, 37
Principles and Practices of Baptist Churches, 62
Principles of Catholic Theology, 25
Proclaiming the Truth, 55
Promise of the Spirit, 35
Prophetic Mysteries Revealed, 31
Proverbs: Personalized Studies for Practical Living, 13
Psalms, The, 13
Psychology for Daily Living, 41
Psychology from a Christian Perspective, 54
Psychology Gone Awry, 53

R

Racial Transition in the Church, 47
Radical Wesley and Patterns for Church Renewal, 63
Rapture Question, The, 31
Rays of Messiah's Glory, 7
Reach Out to Singles, 52
Redemption Truths, 29
Rediscover Your Family Outdoors, 43
Religions of the American Indians, 65
Religious Change and Continuity, 65
Religious Conversion and Personal Identity, 29
Resurrection of Christ, 28
Resurrection of Jesus, 28
Revelation, 23
Revelation of Law in Scripture, 8

Revell's Dictionary of Bible People, 1
Revision Revised, 15
Right Mate, The, 44
Roads a Christian Must Travel, 37
Roots of Modern Mormonism, 65
Royal Dynasties in Ancient Israel, 9
Russell, 63
Ruth, 12

S

Sabbatical Reflections, 33
Sacrificial Worship in the Old Testament, 10
Saint Paul's Epistle to the Ephesians, 21
St. Paul's Epistle to the Thessalonians, 21
Salvation and the Perfect Society, 65
Savior of the World, 19
Scripture Twisting, 66
Search for America's Faith, 47
Secrets for Growing Churches, 48
Secular Humanism, 26
Seed of the Woman, 7
Self–Disclosure, 34
Self–Disclosure, 35
Self–Help Groups for Coping with Crisis, 54
Senior Adult Years, 41
Sermon on the Mount, 19
Sermons, 56
Seven Keys to Maximum Communication, 34
Sex in the World's Religions, 66
Sex Roles and the Christian Family, 40
Sharing Groups in the Church, 54
Shepherding God's Flock, 47
Signals: What Your Child Is Really Telling You, 39
Sinai: The Great and Terrible Wilderness, 9
Sixty–Nine Ways to Start a Study Group and Keep it Growing, 51
Solzhenitsyn: The Moral Vision, 63
Songs of Heaven, 22
Sovereignty of Grace, 26
Spirit of Your Marriage, 43
Spiritual Greatness—Studies in Exodus, 12
Spiritual Nature of Man, 29
Spirituality and the Gentle Life, 37
Stages: Understanding How You Make Your Moral Decisions, 33
Stand Fast in Liberty, 20
Stand Firm in the Faith, 20
Stand United in Joy, 20
Stations of the Mind, 35
Story of King David, 11

Straight Talk to Men and Their Wives, 40
Strategy of Satan, 30
Strike the Original Match, 45
Studies in Genesis, 11
Struggle and Fulfillment, 33
Struggle of Prayer, 34

T

Teenage Rebellion, 40
Teenage Sexuality, 41
Teenagers Ahead, 45
Ten Faces of Ministry, 49
Terminal Care, 53
Text of the Old Testament, 10
That Everyone May Hear, 50
Theme of the Pentateuch, 11
Themes in Old Testament Theology, 9
Theocratic Kingdom of Our Lord Jesus the Christ, 31
Theological Dictionary of the Old Testament, 1
Theological Dynamics, 54
Theological Wordbook of the Old Testament, 2
Theology and Resolution in the Scottish Reformation, 25
Theology of Calvin, 25
Theology of Christian Marriage, 42
Theology of Church Leadership, 52
Theory of Christian Education Practice, 59
Therapy American Style, 54
They Took Themselves Wives, 39
Thoughts on Genesis, 11
Three Steps Forward, Two Steps Back, 37
Toastmaster's Treasure Chest, 56
Today's Tentmakers, 51
Total Image, 36
Total Family, 42
Tradition and Interpretation, 9
Train Up Your Child, 42
Transitions: Making Sense of Life's Changes, 40
Trial of Luther, 63
Trumpet in the Morning, 9
Two Horizons, 16
Two Hundred Years—and Still Counting, 60
Two–Career Marriage, 44

U

Unchurched, The, 47
Unconditional Love, 36
Understanding Church Growth, 57
Understanding Human Values, 36
Understanding Suicide, 53
Understanding the Bible, 5
Understanding Your Past, Key to Your Future, 36
Unity of the Book of Genesis, 11

Unsearchable Riches of Christ, 21
Until We Are Six, 45
Unwanted Generation, 43
Up with Marriage, 43
Use of the Bible in Preaching, 56

V

Values Begin at Home, 46
Van Til: Defender of the Faith, 64
Vision of the Disinherited, 65
Vital Encounter, 18
Vitalizing Intimacy in Marriage, 46

W

Way of the Wilderness, 11
Wedded Unmother, 41
Welcome to the Family, 62
What Ever Happened to the Human Race?, 36
What Every Well–Informed Person Should Know About Drug Addiction, 34
What Should Parents Expect?, 41
What the Bible Teaches About the Bible, 6
What the Bible Teaches About What Jesus Did, 27
What the Cults Believe, 66
What You Should Know About Inerrancy, 6
What's Happening to Clergy Marriages?, 49
Wheeled Vehicles and Ridden Animals in the Ancient Near East, 10
When People Say No, 49
When Your Parents Divorce, 39
Who Art in Heaven, 27
Who Controls Your Child?, 42
Who Dares to Preach?, 55
Who Educates Your Child?, 59
Who is the Ministers' Wife?, 50
Who Needs the Family?, 42
Who's Boss?, 28
Whom Shall I Marry?, 46
Why Believe the Bible?, 6
Why Children Misbehave, 44
William Carey, 63
Win the Battle for Your Mind, 37
Witness to the World, 57
Women and the Word of God, 8
Women of a Certain Age, 44
Word that Kindles, 57
Workaholic and His Family, 43
Working Partners, Working Parents, 40
World Council of Churches and the Demise of Evangelism, 50
Wrestling with Romans, 21
Writers of the New Testament, Their Style and Characteristics, 17
Writings on Christianity and History, 61

Y

Yesterday, Today, and What Next?, 61

You and Your Husband's Mid–Life Crisis, 40

Your Marriage Can Be Great!, 46

Your Marriage Has Real Possibilities, 39

Your Six–Year Old: Defiant but Loving, 39

Youth and Sex, 42

Z

Zechariah and His Prophecies, 14

Zorastrians, 65